D0380955

QUESTIONS
TO ALL YOUR ANSWERS

QUESTIONS
TO ALL YOUR ANSWERS

A JOURNEY FROM FOLK RELIGION TO EXAMINED FAITH

ROGER E. OLSON

ZONDERVAN®

ZONDERVAN.com/
AUTHORTRACKER
follow your favorite authors

ZONDERVAN

Questions to All Your Answers
Copyright © 2007 by the Roger E. Olson

Requests for information should be addressed to:

Zondervan, *Grand Rapids, Michigan* 49530

ISBN 978-0-310-28758-2 (softcover)

Library of Congress Cataloging-in-Publication Data
    Olson, Roger E.
      Questions to all your answers : a journey from folk religion to examined faith /
    Roger E. Olson.
        p. cm.
      Includes bibliographical references.
      1. Apologetics. I. Title.
    BT1103.O47 2006
    230 – dc22   2006022079

All scripture quotations, unless otherwise indicated, are taken from the *Holy Bible, Today's New International Version*™. TNIV®. Copyright © 2001, 2005 by International Bible Society. Used by permission of Zondervan. All rights reserved.

Internet addresses (websites, blogs, etc.) and telephone numbers printed in this book are offered as a resource to you. These are not intended in any way to be or imply an endorsement on the part of Zondervan, nor do we vouch for the content of these sites and numbers for the life of this book.

All rights reserved. No part of this publication may be reproduced, stored in a retrieval system, or transmitted in any form or by any means — electronic, mechanical, photocopy, recording, or any other — except for brief quotations in printed reviews, without the prior permission of the publisher.

Interior design by Nancy Wilson

Printed in the United States of America

To my daughters
Amanda Joy Cox and Sonja Kristen Olson

CONTENTS

FOREWORD

I have to admit something. When I first received the manuscript and looked quickly at the cover and its title, I thought it said, *"Answers to All Your Questions."* I felt a little disappointed and thought to myself, "Oh, no. We really don't need another book that claims to have all the answers." But then I took a second look and realized it didn't say that at all; rather, the title was *"Questions to All Your Answers."* I smiled because I got the play on words and was then thrilled. I thought to myself, "This is great! We need a book like this that will force us to look at what we assume are answers." Within a few seconds, my emotions changed from disappointment to great anticipation.

This title really represents the cry of our hearts. There are plenty of so-called "answers" out there today in the evangelical world. But deep inside we are instinctively beginning to feel that perhaps some of these traditional *answers* aren't always ones we can actually hold with total honesty and full integrity anymore. Perhaps these neat and tidy "answers" were initially accepted because they were taught to us with such confidence that it brought us a sense of security. But over time, we have come to realize that we can't accept these "answers" anymore since they raise even more "questions." We are now able to admit more freely that perhaps many of our "answers" are not quite as clean, final, wrapped up, and packaged as we would like them to be.

What Roger Olson does in this book, then, will help shape the future of the church. He forces us to think and rethink some basic assumptions we have had about some significant and practical life issues. We definitely do need books on worship, leadership, ecclesiology, and the mission of the church. But as we are on this mission, we will no doubt need to face hard questions that we can't hide from or ignore. These are the questions today's culture is asking; we can no longer settle for simplistic answers of "folk religion," as Roger puts it. That is why a book like this is so important for the future church. It will help us think about the answers we have received to our questions as well as think about the questions that come from our answers.

What I so admire about Roger Olson being the author of this book is that he isn't afraid to question the "folk religion answers." We may not all admit we have thought about these answers and questioned them, but I bet most of us have. Yet Roger isn't doing this with any sense of shallowness but with great heart and depth. He is a scholar who obviously understands people. With this understanding, he is able to guide us through various ways to rethink some of the popular answers that may not be as cut and dried as we originally thought them to be.

What I love about this book is that it will cause us to think about some common Christian clichés — clichés so familiar to us that we haven't stopped to pay deeper attention to what they are really saying or if they truly make sense. This book is a wonderful mix of being challenged to use our minds and think theologically, but also to grasp how our thinking matters in our basic day-to-day living. Roger challenges us to look at how we have turned complex theological issues into standard Christian responses such as "God is in control," "Jesus is the answer," and "the Bible has all the answers." These may sound nice, but they really are more "folk religion" than true questions of examined faith.

This book will truly cause your mind to grow. But it isn't just about growth and being stretched in your thinking. Roger has written a book that will help your heart and mind worship more purely and think more clearly. As a result of this, your walk with Jesus will be deeper and richer, which in turn will enable the Spirit of God to use you all the more on the mission he has given to each one of us.

Dan Kimball, author, *The Emerging Church*
(*www.vintagefaith.com*)

This book is written with a pastoral heart. What I mean is that its purpose is spiritual formation, including correction of bad theology. One of my basic presuppositions is that God cares what we think about him and how we interpret and communicate the faith. God has given us a pretty large book known as the Bible because he wants us to know him, and that implies thinking right thoughts about him.

Can we ever get the faith totally right? I don't think so. We are finite and fallen, so there will always be some element of distortion in our best attempts to understand and articulate the gospel. But that doesn't excuse sloppy Christian thinking, let alone no Christian thinking at all! The pastoral concern driving this little book is that far too many contemporary evangelical Christians have succumbed to what sociologists of religion call "folk religion." I'll sometimes refer to it more specifically as "folk Christianity." It's a badly distorted version of Christianity that thrives on clichés and slogans and resists reflection and examination. Too often I hear that we are not to "question God." Perhaps. But surely

> **CAN** we ever get the faith totally right? I don't think so. We're finite and fallen so there will always be some element of distortion in our best attempts to understand and articulate the gospel. But that doesn't excuse sloppy Christian thinking let alone no Christian thinking at all!

we are to question our own and others' ideas about God and the messages about God and spirituality that float around in culture (including Christian culture).

Paul urged the Thessalonian Christians faced with various spiritual messages to "test them all" (1 Thessalonians 5:21), meaning to examine the messages of prophets and others who claimed to speak for God or about God. We've become too relaxed about this, perhaps because our culture resists "judging." (This is something we'll discuss at length in chapter 9.) It seems judgmental to test and examine people's spiritual messages. But why? They can't all be true, can they? Certainly not. Many flatly contradict each other. Only the worst kind of fuzzy-headed postmodernism (which is really postmodern culture gone to seed!) embraces everything. In fact, I doubt that kind of universal acceptance of all truth claims is even possible. But we do encounter it occasionally.

> **THE** unexamined faith is not worth believing.

After I gave a talk on Shirley MacLaine and the New Age Movement some years ago, a well-meaning Christian came up to me and said, "You know, reincarnation can be true for her even if it's not true for you." My response was simply an incredulous look at this educated man. What does that even mean? I knew him well enough to know that he wasn't just mouthing the truism that people have different perceptions of truth.

Most of the time on our best days we all know that some messages in culture and the church are good and others not so good. Try an experiment. Watch a selection of programs on religious television networks. Or browse the shelves of any Christian bookstore. I think you'll quickly find a lot of variety and much questionable material. And yet many contemporary Christians think it is okay and even spiritual to swallow it all hook, line, and sinker! If Paul were alive today I'm sure he'd say to them, "Test them all."

Socrates is supposed to have said "The unexamined life is not worth living." A Christian philosopher paraphrased Socrates: "The unexamined faith is not worth believing." Many Christians will shudder at such a statement. Why? Because evangelical pietism (which often is really pietism gone to seed) revels in "heart religion" focused almost exclusively on feelings and acts of the will, with little or no intellectual content. Somehow we've equated hard thinking about the faith with lack of spiritual fervor.

Have you ever wondered what Paul would think about that? He seemed to revel in questioning the popular messages of other church leaders (most of whose names we don't know). His letters abound in examining the faith of others, and sometimes he even questioned his own grasp of gospel truth. But most tellingly, he applauded a

WE do God no favors by being gullible, credulous, irrational, or uncritical. God gave us minds and expects us to use them.

group of people at Berea for examining his message to them and not simply swallowing it whole. Our folk evangelicalism too often denigrates the life of the mind and especially critical thinking. Even to raise an honest question about a popularly believed evangelegend (religious urban legend) is enough to provoke prayers on your behalf for your spiritual renewal.

This is not as it should be. We do God no favors by being gullible, credulous, irrational, or uncritical. God gave us minds and expects us to use them. No special spiritual aura accompanies stupidity or ignorance. The ancient icon of the "holy fool" is unbiblical. When Paul wrote to the Corinthians about the "foolishness of the cross," he was simply contrasting the true gospel with the Gnostics' allegedly more sophisticated version. He did not intend to encourage sacrifice of the intellect or holy ignorance. All too often, however, contemporary popular Christianity leads people to think that spirituality and hard thinking stand in conflict with each other.

FOLK RELIGION AND FOLK CHRISTIANITY

Folk religion is the result of pietism gone to seed. Pietism was originally a good movement to renew and revive authentic Christianity among European and later American Protestant congregations. It arose in Germany in the seventeenth century and focused attention on the "inner man" as the seat of God's work of transforming a person's life. It aimed to correct undue attention to the intellect and "dead orthodoxy" by emphasizing spiritual experience and even feelings for God.

Over the centuries, however, a degenerate form of pietism has invaded the evangelical subculture. The original Pietists, such as Philipp Spener, August Hermann Francke, and Nikolaus Ludwig von Zinzendorf, would hardly recognize their legacy in contemporary evangelicalism. These men did not shy away from education and the life of the mind or from critical thinking; they only wanted to add a stronger note of spirituality and inwardness to Protestantism. Too many of their contemporary heirs have fallen into an extremely informal, individualized, anti-intellectual form of Christianity that eschews mental exercise of the faith.

Folk religion thrives on clichés and slogans that fit on bumper stickers and resists their critical examination even by the litmus test of Scripture. It revolves around cute or comforting sayings drawn from choruses, church marquees, and devotional books. It elevates to canonical status fascinating spiritual stories passed around orally or on the internet. Above all it resists any attempt to subject these to critical scrutiny.

Some years ago a story about well drillers discovering hell and hearing the cries coming up from the depths was invented and circulated by a skeptic. His purpose was apparently to demonstrate how gullible religious people can be. It worked. Some of my own relatives, friends, and students read the tale in Christian publications (and later on the internet) and insisted on its truth even in the face of total lack of evidence. This is an example of what folklorists call an evangelegend. Even when the inventor of the story finally admitted fabricating it and a major evangelical periodical exposed it as untrue, many Christians refused to stop circulating it. Many Christians spend more time reading such stories on the internet than reading their Bibles.

Folk Christianity is the specifically Christian form of folk religion. Every world religion has its folk manifestations. Some religions exist only as folk religion. An example is astrology (although I suppose some astrologers might object). A folk religion has little or no scholarly or intellectual tradition and is practiced mostly by individuals although they may network with each other. A folk religion spawns little or no research and focused thought. Theology is anathema to folk religion; it lives by word of mouth and internet circulation. It cares only about feelings and experiences and hardly at all about doctrine or critical reflection.

> FOLK religion thrives on clichés and slogans that fit on bumper stickers and resists their critical examination even by the litmus test of Scripture.

Folk Christianity consists of a common stock of cute or comforting sayings and sweet aphorisms worked into and out of songs, poems, and devotional books. Everyone has heard the maxim that "God helps those who help themselves." It's a perfect example of folk religion, and it has entered into folk Christianity. Many Christians believe that it's in the Bible! One well-known evangelist quipped that if it isn't in the Bible it should be! In fact, it isn't in the Bible, and it contradicts historic Christian doctrine that emphasizes the priority and primacy of grace even over our first exercise of a goodwill toward God. (Chapter 6 will discuss the primacy of grace in detail.)

Folk Christianity has existed as long as Christianity itself. It can be found behind the New Testament texts themselves. Apparently some of the apostles' writings were aimed at correcting popular beliefs that arose among their first converts. The apostle who wrote the epistle to the Hebrews challenged his readers to go beyond the milk of the Word to its meat, by which he meant they should transcend their childish ideas to spiritual maturity—just as he had. The sixteenth-century Catholic Reformer Desiderius Erasmus specialized in satirizing folk Christianity in Europe. He ridiculed the masses' pilgrimages to kiss relics of saints, including their belief in gallons of the Virgin Mary's milk all over the continent. His dialogues between equally gullible and piously devout pilgrims to the holy shrines still stand as models of religious satire.

But the real heyday of modern evangelical folk Christianity seems to have been the late 1960s and early 1970s with the rise of the Jesus People movement. Anyone who lived through that period and participated in that Christian hippie phenomenon can attest to its extreme informality, anti-traditionalism, and anti-intellectualism. Jesus freaks, as many Jesus People liked to be called, reveled in overturning old religious habits, breaking old spiritual wineskins, and democratizing the faith. It was the most populist Christian movement since the early Quakers.

Many Jesus People went on to study theology and teach in evangelical Christian colleges and seminaries; some became Episcopalians or Eastern Orthodox believers. The search for roots and solid theological ground beneath their feet was a natural reaction to the movement's extreme rejection of everything cerebral, liturgical, and theological. But the Jesus People movement was the quintessential folk religious phenomenon. It thrived on passion and ardor to the exclusion of critical thinking. It was a wonderful and heady swell of spiritual passion, but it left many of us longing for something more solid than inward movings of the Holy Spirit. Like many other Jesus People, I discovered Francis Schaeffer's books and began to examine critically the subjectivism of super-spirituality and to look for answers that satisfied the head as well as the heart. Later I became somewhat disillusioned with Schaeffer's high Calvinism and extremely negative assessment of Western culture. But he played an important role in bringing many of us to a more examined and reflective faith.

However, the intensely subjective spirituality of the Jesus People movement seeped into the mainstream of American evangelical life. Chorus singing replaced hymns, and many evangelicals ran from anything that smacked of tradition, liturgy, or theology. People who never heard of the Jesus People movement are still under its influence; churches that once despised the shoeless, long-haired, guitar-playing Jesus People as fanatics now sing their songs ("I Wish We'd All Been Ready"), repeat their clichés ("There's no trip like Jesus!"), and, like them, denigrate denominations and theology ("religious head trip"). The problem is that the Jesus People movement, for all the good it did, spawned numerous cults that taught all manner of heresies and condoned if not encouraged sexual deviance and spiritual abuse.

So folk Christianity, which has been around in some form as long as Christianity itself, received a big boost from the Jesus People movement of the 1960s and 1970s. It has become part and parcel of the American evangelical scene. What's wrong with that? Well, as I just mentioned, the Jesus People movement lacked the doctrinal discernment to prevent all manner of heresies and deviance from occurring and spinning off into numerous cults, sects, and weird communes. Most of that was repetitious of earlier heresies that the church fathers and Reformers dealt with long ago. If the leaders of the Jesus People movement had known more about Christian history, they may have been able to recognize what was happening and correct it right away. But they were trying to reinvent Christianity from the ground up, as if two thousand years of Christian tradition had never happened or wasn't even worth studying.

Furthermore, Jesus People folk religion led many to disconnect their spiritual lives from the world around them; they preached at

> TO the extent that Christianity is reduced to folk religion, it ghettoizes itself from the wider culture and fails to be an influence in the public square.

the masses without even attempting to offer intelligible answers or explanations to inquiring minds (until later when some became rabid apologists for the faith). Folk religion avoids putting spirituality into intelligible expression; it eschews reasonable answers and underscores feelings as the only foundation for faith. It thereby loses its public voice. *To the extent that Christianity is reduced to folk religion, it ghettoizes itself from the wider culture and fails to be an influence in the public square.*

EXAMINED, REFLECTIVE FAITH

So what is the alternative and antidote to folk Christianity? If Christianity is to regain its objective status as a great tradition of culture-influencing spiritual and theological power, what must happen? I'm not recommending that evangelicals or anyone else abandon the intense spirituality of pietism or the Jesus People movement. These were valuable correctives to dead orthodoxy and formalism. Christians were right to object most strenuously to the nominal Christianity that identified itself with a doctrinal system or with creedalism or denominationalism. But folk religion is not the only alternative to these, and it is a dangerous alternative. It reduces Christianity to the social status of astrology—a private belief system with no prophetic voice to the wider culture. Robust, public, influential Christianity needs an intellectual side, and an intellectual side is impossible without critical thought.

> FOLK religion reduces Christianity to the social status of astrology—a private belief system with no prophetic voice to the wider culture. Robust, public, influential Christianity needs an intellectual side, and an intellectual side is impossible without critical thought.

But isn't critical thinking antithetical to real spirituality? Even the predictability of that question reveals how far we have gone in the direction of folk religion. Almost no Christian leader before the late twentieth century would say so. But now it has virtually become an operating presupposition among evangelical Christians that critical examination and questioning of religious and spiritual messages labeled "Christian" is bad.

"Test them all." That was Paul's imperative to first-century Christians. Apparently Paul wanted the Thessalonians to include critical thinking in their arsenal of weapons of spiritual warfare. How odd that sounds today—critical thinking as a weapon of spiritual warfare. But why not? It's biblical. It's necessary in the contemporary spiritual marketplace where everything from spiritualism (communicating with the dead) to religious racism ("Christian Identity") to belief in reincarnation is being included under the heading "Christian varieties."

I attended a public speech by the Rev. Sun Myung Moon of Korea and sadly observed a Baptist minister deliver the invocation just before the man many of his followers consider the "Lord of the Second Advent" came on stage to speak. I know of a Baptist church in a major Northeastern city where the pastor channels the spirits of "dearly departed" church members who give messages to the congregation. In these days the response of too many is "That's different" rather than "That's wrong." The only antidote is a recovery of *reflective Christianity*.

Reflective Christianity is the opposite of folk religion. It values the life of the mind and critical thought. It encourages spiritual people to add head to heart and develop critical discernment skills. It calls on Christians to learn not only the Bible but also the great tradition of Christian thought throughout the ages and to study doctrine and philosophy even if only as dabblers. It values asking tough questions about stories that sound like legends and clichés that try to put the gospel into a cute nutshell. It is not afraid of charges of being unspiritual as it confidently forges ahead in examining the faith under the guiding lodestar of God's Word, using reason as a resource and necessary tool.

Reflective Christianity has the courage to say "I don't know," *rather than fall back on half-baked and pat answers that wither and die under scrutiny.* It admits that now, this side of heaven, we all see through a glass darkly (as Paul admitted to the Corinthians) and therefore lack absolute certainty and pithy, pat responses when it comes to hard questions about evil, suffering, life after death, the fate of the unevangelized, and many, many more controverted subjects. It knows that sometimes we have to live with questions that have no absolute, definite answers but that using our God-given minds to search out and discover answers is a Christian vocation. It respects careful, reasonable, culturally sensitive Christian thinkers like C. S. Lewis, G. K. Chesterton, Lesslie Newbigin, and Harry Blamires. It has little use for those brash and triumphalist apologists who use demagoguery to bash as stupid or unspiritual everyone who thinks differently.

Reflective Christianity is mature, wise Christian spirituality. It takes a dim view of anti-intellectualism and obscurantism. One evangelical pastor concluded his sermon on "The Christian Response to Culture" by saying, "The Christian's response to those who challenge our faith is 'Don't confuse me with the facts; my mind is already made up.' " A nice old Christian man took me aside as I left to study theology in Germany and said, "Roger, remember that there is such a thing as an overeducated idiot."

Unlike folk Christianity, *reflective Christianity encourages and enables education and is not afraid of facts.* It believes that authentic Christian faith can stand up to the scrutiny of close, critical examination. And what can't stand up should fall down. Of course, that doesn't mean whatever can't stand up to secular reasoning imbued with the spirit of naturalism (anti-supernatural philosophy) should fall down. Naturalism and secularism are not facts; they are worldviews. Reflective Christianity is willing to put real Christianity up against those and trust its power to attract and persuade. It does not run and hide behind a fortress of feel-good spirituality and religious groupthink when the winds of science and philosophy blow against it. It studies, interprets, thinks, examines, and refines even its own expressions in order to make them intelligible to the seekers of the world.

Reflective Christianity values Christian roots; it admires and respects the great sages of the Christian past. Without putting the church fathers or the Reformers on a pedestal as if they were prophets or apostles, it sits at their feet to learn their wisdom. Sometimes it has to disagree with them on some points. That's as it should be. They were not supernaturally inspired. But they are our ancestors in the faith who handed it down to us, and for that they should be remembered and respected.

Reflective Christianity is catholic Christianity. Not necessarily Roman Catholic but catholic in the sense of thinking and worshiping along with the great cloud of witnesses of all the ages — men and women of faith who suffered and died for the faith and who left a deposit of writings saturated in the blood, sweat, and tears of years of undying devotion to and study of God's Word. Reflective Christianity is rooted in Christian tradition; it is not Lone Ranger spirituality reinventing the wheel of the faith.

Reflective Christianity is reasonable Christianity. It does not run from logic or evidence but uses them in the service of the King. It regards the mind and nature as works of God. It knows them to be fallen and therefore not entirely trustworthy, but it also sees them as redeemable and therefore realms of mercy and grace when submitted to the lordship of Jesus Christ. Reflective Christianity does not fly in the face of brute facts of science or mock serious philosophy and other intellectual endeavors. It absorbs the whole world and struggles to integrate it with the gospel. It is holistic rather than dualistic in its approach to faith and life; it seeks to connect spirituality and business, faith and research, God's Word and social life.

Reflective Christianity is humble because it knows how little we really know or understand about the great mysteries of God and the universe. The fault is not God's or the universe's but ours. Because of our finitude and fallenness we cannot know or understand many things. We have to learn to live with questions and embrace mystery. But it strictly eschews contradictions and is uncomfortable with paradoxes. It regards a paradox (an apparent contradiction) in religion as a task for thought. Rather than simply playing the mystery card too early, reflective Christianity is willing to think and think again about hard problems presented by God's Word.

Chapter 1 will focus on this theme and thesis. While God's Word is not opaque, the sinful blinders on our eyes keep us from understanding it as well as we should. But the mind is one instrument God has provided for understanding better. Yet, reflective Christianity is comfortable with ambiguity if not with paradox. Black and white, either-or thinking is childish and immature. There are gray areas in spirituality, morality, and ethics as well as in doctrine. The very best Christian minds have struggled to explain the problem of evil, to justify the ways of God in the face of the horrors of history and natural calamities. Reflective Christianity may settle for one approach as better than others, but it knows and admits that every answer has some problems.

What's good about reflective Christianity? In a word — it's mature Christianity. To ask what's good about it is like asking what's good about growing up mentally and emotionally. It comes with its unique pains, but who thinks growing up is bad? Reflective Christianity is wise Christianity. It's what God calls us to. Paul urged his converts to grow up in Christ and stop thinking and acting as children. He challenged them to get themselves prepared for the solid meat of doctrine and leave behind their diets of milk, which probably meant spiritually "lite" and pleasing teachings.

But perhaps most important of all, reflective Christianity is culture-shaping Christianity. It encounters the world and presents the Christian message as a viable competitor against all the other worldviews and philosophies and spiritualities in the marketplace of ideas. It is unafraid of the hard task of critically thinking through and sometimes against what is already believed and taught and making it intelligible to honest seekers after truth. It is also self-critical Christianity that does not make idols out of traditional beliefs or personal feelings or favorite styles of worship but subjects them all to the test of truth and lets the chips fall where they may.

REFLECTIVE Christianity is culture-shaping Christianity.

For reflective Christianity, the only ultimate authority is truth itself. It agrees with the sage Samuel Taylor Coleridge, who said that the man who loves Christianity more than truth will go on to love his own denomination more than Christianity and end up loving himself more than anything. Truth is what we are after, and we believe God is truth and has given us Jesus Christ as our truth. Reflective Christians do not sing the old gospel hymn "If I Am Dreaming, Let Me Dream On." Illusion is not good; truth is better than every nice dream. We are Christians because we believe Christianity is the path to truth, not because it is our escape from reality or truth.

A CASE STUDY OF REFLECTIVE FAITH

Reflective Christianity is somewhat disillusioned Christianity. It knows that many tough questions of faith have no pat answers and that many of the simplistic answers often touted by folk Christianity are too shallow to do justice to the great mysteries and depths of the faith. Many evangelicals grew up hearing that "my God can do anything" (the title of at least one popular chorus of the '60s) and similar clichés. They and most of their cohort of evangelical young people assumed this meant God can literally do anything without exceptions, qualifications, or limits. Throughout my twenty-some years of full-time theology teaching in Christian higher education I've met many an evangelical pastor's son or daughter who wanted to defend this idea with determined resolution. It isn't that this saying has no truth value at all. All trite little clichés have some truth. The problem is that they pretend to be the whole truth and people take them too literally. Reflective Christianity has confronted the exceptions to "my God can do anything" and (perhaps) kept on singing the chorus anyway. But mature evangelical leaders want to help Christian youth realize that things are a little more complex than at first appears to be the case.

> **ALL** trite little clichés have some truth. The problem is that they pretend to be the whole truth and people take them too literally.

I have always had an inquiring mind. I had the advantage of being raised by a father who was both an evangelical pastor for fifty-three years and a person of uncommon sense and natural ability to think critically. Whether from my father or from teachers or both, I picked up the habit of questioning trite sayings and shallow answers. Throughout my four years at a fundamentalist college I gained a reputation as a skeptic merely for asking questions and pushing my teachers and classmates to think about the problems involved in their beliefs. My intention was never to be destructive; I just knew that some of what was being promoted as sound and solid Christian belief was pretty shaky unless it could be carefully nuanced and qualified in the right ways.

Take "my God can do anything," for example. I don't remember when it first occurred to me to ask whether God can change the past. But many people to whom I posed the question responded after a moment's reflection that he can't. The past is what is already done and can't be changed. Then is it true that "my God can do anything"? Others quickly pronounced, "Of course! My God can do anything. Sorry about yours." But then I asked them, "When was the last time you prayed and asked God to undo something terrible that has already happened?" Many just looked at me quizzically and walked away. Others said, "Only *you* would think of something like that!" But some said, "Well, that's a good question" and began to think about God's limitations.

It seems to me that if God could change the past, the Bible would encourage God's people to pray for God to do just that. At least there would be stories of it happening. Besides, in spite of all the movies about time travel (i.e., "back to the future"), the very notion of changing the past is counterintuitive, to say the least. One alteration of the past would have enormous ramifications for the present. This would then be a different world. A person who believes God can and does change the past would need to think through some of these issues and be prepared to give some kind of reasonable response. The difficulty has led even the most conservative evangelical scholars to deny that God can change the past. They then know, whether they admit it or not, that "My God can do anything" needs some qualifications. Can God sin? Can God break his promises? Can God commit suicide? Can God coerce free agents such as we are (according to many evangelicals)? Such questions may sound like a mere mind game, but honest, seeking, open-minded inquirers into Christianity will want answers to such questions.

GOOD QUESTIONING

The point is that mature, reflective Christianity (which is always a work in progress and never a finished product) will at least acknowledge the problems of some of these Christian clichés, seek the right opportunities to probe into them, and find ways to express the truth about God's power in a faithful and reasonable manner. A mature, reflective Christian is not in the habit of going around getting into other people's faces with such questions. I was immature during my college years although I still think it was appropriate to ask my teachers such questions. My immaturity showed in my tendency to confront fellow students and well-meaning church folks with them.

Reflective Christianity is not about chronic skepticism or showing off one's ability to demolish trite sayings; it is about developing the

> **REFLECTIVE** Christianity is not about chronic skepticism or showing off one's ability to demolish trite sayings; it is about developing the ability to gently take people to a deeper level of understanding about God and the faith while respecting their hearts.

ability to gently take people to a deeper level of understanding about God and the faith while respecting their hearts. German theologian Helmut Thielicke's little book *A Little Exercise for Young Theologians* (Eerdmans, 1972) presents a model for this respectful reflective Christianity; it contains great wisdom from an older theologian to younger ones. And all who think reflectively about faith are theologians even if they never think of themselves that way.

Someone has said that reflective Christianity involves questioning what you believe while continuing to believe what you are questioning. That's kind of like walking on a tightrope. How can I believe and question what I believe at the same time? I once heard a sermon by an evangelical youth evangelist on "It's Time to Believe Our Beliefs and Doubt Our Doubts." Well, that's okay for thirteen-year-olds. And it's fairly easy—especially for those surrounded by people of their own faith. But it does little for Christian inquiring minds preparing to enter the wider pluralistic world of contemporary secular and pagan society. Somehow we need to develop the ability to go on believing basic Christian truths while questioning their formulations and especially folk religious clichés and evangelegends.

This process will inevitably involve some level of cognitive dissonance—the experience of having cherished beliefs challenged by trusted people. That's what this book is about. I realize that I may not be "trusted" by many readers. But perhaps my years of teaching in evangelical Christian colleges and universities (and now a seminary) will create some amount of trust. *Be assured that I am a committed evangelical.* I have no intention of destroying anyone's evangelical faith. I would like to see more evangelicals move beyond simplistic ways of believing and beyond folk Christianity to a higher, deeper, and more mature faith. One way to do that is to raise hard questions about some of the most popular sayings deeply cherished by Christians stuck in folk religion. But this purpose is not a destructive one; it is to help people develop a more mature, reasonable, and properly nuanced Christian faith that is still

> **REFLECTIVE** Christianity involves questioning what you believe while continuing to believe what you are questioning.

rooted and grounded in the soil of biblical revelation and historic Christianity.

To that end I have identified ten popular beliefs that seem to me seriously problematic. These are popular beliefs that endure over time. I'm not interested here in attacking this week's Christian legend circulating on the internet. I've chosen ten beliefs that I have found prevalent among students at Christian colleges and universities and too often among youth pastors and even pastors of churches (to say nothing of people in the pews!). Each one of them is, I believe, fraught with difficulties as it stands. Of course, many people who say these things have thought about them critically but returned to them with good reasons. That's fine. But my experience is that such people who are on the path to mature, reflective Christian faith never say them in quite the same way after examining them. They usually qualify them with exceptions or cautious explanations. Not one of these ten popular Christian sayings expresses something essential to the gospel itself; they are all problematic expressions of doctrines and when properly qualified they communicate a truth. But more often than not they are misleading.

One final word before we plunge into this exercise. My purpose here is not merely to raise questions about ten particular items of evangelical folk religion. It is rather to model one aspect of reflective Christianity—critically examining unexamined popular folk religious beliefs in order to go deeper into the mysteries of the faith. The purpose is to demonstrate how complicated some Christian beliefs really are and how they deserve deeper thought and understanding than many Christians give them. Ultimately, my purpose is to help Christians express their beliefs in intelligible ways that open but critically minded, thinking inquirers can hear and accept.

An example not among the ten chosen for this little book is the almost universal folk Christian explanation of the Trinity as belief that God is "three in one, one in three." Of course, this is drawn largely from hymns and spiritual songs that do not have the space to express the mystery of the Trinity adequately. But to stop there is misleading. Inquiring minds naturally want to know "*three* what and *one* what?" Is the Trinity a sheer logical or mathematical contradiction? Of course not. But too many evangelicals mired in folk Christianity present it that way. The early church fathers explained that God is three "persons" (*hypostases*) and one "substance" (*ousia*). He is not three persons and one person or one substance and three substances. Thus, there is no real contradiction involved in the real doctrine of the Trinity. But folk Christianity often presents the doctrine as if it requires a sacrifice of logic.

My hope and prayer is that readers (and reviewers!) will approach this book with a hermeneutic of charity. That is, understand that it is not intended to destroy anyone's faith. Its only intention is a pastoral one—to help maturing Christians move on to a deeper level of understanding and expressing the common faith we all share as followers of Jesus Christ.

DISCUSSION QUESTIONS

1. Do you think it is possible to arrive at a complete and correct theology that never needs revision? Why or why not?

2. Do you agree that the unexamined faith is not worth believing? Why or why not?

3. Where do you see folk religion in culture and church life? What are some specific examples?

4. How important is it for Christian witness and belief to be coherent and intelligible? What are some problems with striving and not striving for it?

5. Do you think there are "things" God cannot do (e.g., change the past)? What are some other examples of things God cannot do? Or do you think God can perform whatever task humans can conceive for him to do? Why?

6. What elements of folk religion can you recognize in your own faith?

7. What concerns or attracts you at this point about the prospect of developing examined, reflective Christian faith? Are you open to this? Do you have any fears or hesitations? What are they? What appeals to you about it?

CHAPTER 1

IT'S A MYSTERY, JUST ACCEPT IT:

SO WHAT DO YOU SAY TO AN ATHEIST?

A group of young Christians is sitting in a circle discussing a challenging problem in Christian belief. Perhaps it's the Trinity or maybe predestination and free will. Or it could be the divinity and humanity of Jesus Christ. After a brief back and forth about the topic during which someone offers up a pretty deep theological concept such as "hypostatic union" (that Jesus Christ is one person with two distinct natures), another person says, "Hey! It's a mystery, just accept it as such and don't think so hard."

Usually this contribution to the discussion is uttered at the point where the sledding in theology gets a little tough. Minds are being stretched. Various devout theories of how the mind can wrap itself around a tough Christian belief are being discussed. But just as the discussion gets interesting, someone opens the anti-intellectual hatch and jumps down into the pit of obscurantism. Instead of appealing to mystery they might say, "It's a paradox! Just embrace it as such." You may not see this cliché on any pious bumper sticker, but a lot of folk Christians say it in some form when they don't want to use their minds (or don't like it that others have used their minds) to wrestle with difficult problems presented to us by divine revelation in Scripture.

Again, please don't get me wrong. I'm not saying that appeal to mystery or paradox is necessarily always a bad thing. A mystery may simply be something beyond human comprehension, so there are aspects of God that are mysterious. A paradox is an apparent contradiction; it is when two things are equally affirmed and yet we cannot see how they can both be true. A famous example from physics is light—it appears to have the qualities of waves and of particles, and yet physicists do not know how that's possible. Until a more complete model is constructed, light will just have to be thought of as both wave-like and particle-like even though that involves an apparent contradiction. But notice the "until some more complete model is constructed" part of that sentence. Scientists don't sit easily or comfortably with paradox because contradiction is always a sign of something wrong in reasonable discourse. Even an apparent contradiction is a problem.

> **RATHER** than jump too quickly and comfortably into appeal to mystery or embrace of paradox, perhaps we should consider all the possibilities and use our God-given minds to think long and hard about where the mystery truly lies, whether paradox is really necessary, and whether there might be a way to relieve it that is both faithful and reasonable.

I like to tell my students that a paradox is always a task for further thought—even in theology. Rather than jump too quickly and comfortably into appeal to mystery or embrace of paradox, perhaps we should consider all the possibilities and use our God-given minds to think long and hard about where the mystery truly lies, whether paradox is really necessary (or the result of some misunderstanding), and whether there might be a way to relieve it that is both faithful and reasonable.

PARADOX, MYSTERY, AND AMERICAN CULTURE

Some educated readers might be wondering about the great Danish Christian philosopher Søren Kierkegaard (1813–1855). He encouraged recognition of paradox in Christian theology. Was he into folk religion? Hardly. Kierkegaard was reacting to another philosopher—G. W. F. Hegel of Germany (1770–1831). Hegel believed and taught that the human mind is capable of using reason to resolve all paradoxes in syntheses of truths. For him, philosophy and logic can think God's own thoughts after him because there's a basic continuity between human reason (at its best) and God's mind. A favorite saying of Hegel's was, "The real is the rational."

Kierkegaard believed that Hegel and his followers were sucking the life out of Christianity by reducing it to a rational philosophical system. The mystery was being destroyed. And since God is wholly other than us, there will always be mysteries surrounding God, and our best attempts to think about God will be expressed in paradoxes. But none of this means that Kierkegaard flew into appeal to mystery or paradox in order to avoid the hard work of using his mind to think about God and God's revelation of himself in Scripture. He was a genius and put his intellect to work to study philosophy and theology.

In my opinion, appeal to mystery and paradox is a problem in spite of Kierkegaard's genius. The problem with appeal to mystery is when it happens too soon. I doubt Kierkegaard was as guilty of this as many people think. But he did like to underline and highlight the transcendence (wholly otherness) of God, which led him to value the role of mystery in Christian thinking. Many contemporary Christians think they can and perhaps should simply lump all Christian doctrines into the "mystery box" and avoid inspecting them with their minds to see if it may be possible to penetrate part way into their meanings. As I will explain later, appeal to mystery is justified—but only after we have used our God-given intellects to the best of our abilities (even to the point where our heads hurt a little!) to examine and understand what God has revealed. Some people jump to mystery too fast and too soon and thereby risk making Christianity sound esoteric (secret, hidden knowledge) rather than public and intelligible.

> SOME people jump to mystery too fast and too soon and thereby risk making Christianity sound esoteric rather than public and intelligible.

The problems with the appeal to paradox are like the problems with appealing to mystery. First, like premature appeal to mystery, appeal to paradox is problematic when people do it to avoid mental exertion in the service of understanding God's Word. Second, it's disturbing when people embrace paradox as a sign of spirituality and denigrate the ongoing task of making the Christian message intelligible. In other words, appeal to paradox is bad when it is a sign of anti-intellectualism or sheer mental laziness. At the end of a long road of careful study and consideration, reflective Christianity might end up affirming about some revealed truth that "It's a paradox," as a recognition of mystery. But it will always be after every effort toward coherence has been exhausted. And it will be an uncomfortable admission with the intention of pursuing the matter further when more light is available.

To be perfectly honest with you, I am not entirely happy about Kierkegaard or his high reputation among many evangelicals. That's not because I think he was a heretic or anything like that. I certainly respect him as a prophet who stood alone against the tidal wave of cultural Christianity that swamped the gospel in Europe in his time. But I think he overreacted to Hegel. Hegel himself was perhaps only overreacting to someone else who he thought was separating faith and reason too much (e.g., the German philosopher Immanuel Kant). Could there be some truth in both Kierkegaard and Hegel?

In any case, contemporary evangelical Christians too often jump on the paradox bandwagon without even attempting to learn whether constructive theology might have a possible solution to a problem that arises out of Scripture. Why? America is an instrumentalist society. I once had a professor who complained that all American public schools are "John Dewey schools." It took some digging to figure out what he meant. John Dewey was a secular philosopher who taught that humans are problem-solving animals. (Not to say that he intended to reduce human beings to animals, but without a supernatural worldview that does seem to be inevitable.) We seek to solve problems, and "truth" is what works to do that. His philosophy was a form of pragmatism that he called instrumentalism. It resonated with a lot of people in America; something in our collective psyche drives us to value practical things and shy away from speculation, thought for thought's sake, abstract ideas. We want to know the "cash value" of an idea before we think it important. So, Dewey's ideas were enthusiastically embraced by secular people and eventually seeped into Christianity (as culture has a tendency to do).

Like our secular neighbors, American Christians are profoundly pragmatic. We're pragmatic even about our spirituality and theology. I can testify to that based on years of teaching theology. When confronted with an idea about God most Christians want to know, "What is its cash value?" They may not ask it in quite so crass a way, but their concern is with how ideas work to benefit them or someone else. Sometimes I just say, "Well, perhaps God just cares what we think about him whether it has any practical benefit or not." That seems like a radically new idea to many people, and few are ready to accept it without some convincing. Not all cultures are so pragmatic about ideas; some European cultures have a long history of intellectual inquiry regardless of practical value. But we Americans are conditioned to think there's something wrong with believing things without seeing some short-term consequences.

My point in all this is simply that the tendency of American Christians to play the "mystery card" or the "paradox card" quickly in theological discussions may have something to do with our bias against ideas that don't feel like tools. In other words, if we can't see what to do with an idea, we would rather not play around with it; we prefer to just put it down. One way to do that is to say, "It's a mystery," or "It's a paradox," and refuse to think further. And we are easily and quickly frustrated with people who do put their minds to work trying to relieve a paradox. Our question is "Why bother?" "Don't think so much; just affirm what you're supposed to and let it go!"

I should stop here and make perfectly clear that this all-too-common response to intellectual endeavor in spiritual and theological matters is different from that of someone who has worked hard at solving a theological dilemma and relieving paradox and yet found it impossible. Such Christian intellectuals and writers are not necessarily folk Christians. So, once again, the cliché is only evidence of folk religion in Christian life in a certain context—when it is an excuse not to think but a flight from using the mind to understand God's self-revelation in Jesus Christ and Scripture.

GOOD MYSTERY

Another caveat is in order. I'm not against appeal to mystery in every case. The great French existentialist Christian Gabriel Marcel (1889–1973) made a distinction between a problem and a mystery. Some issues are problems to be solved while others are mysteries to be embraced. Embracing mystery is not necessarily a bad thing. I gladly embrace mystery after doing my work of thinking hard and long about the meaning of God's revelation because God is beyond complete comprehension. There are aspects to God I will never understand because God is God and I am not. That's the fundamental Christian attitude that underlies everything else. God is transcendent, which means "wholly other" than anything he creates even if creation reflects something of himself. Even with our best spiritual-intellectual efforts we will never fully understand all there is to being God. God is simply too deep for us.

However, too many Christians know all too well that the Bible says God's ways are not our ways and his thoughts are not our thoughts (Isaiah 55:8–9). It's true, of course. But we shouldn't use it as license to stop trying to understand God using the clues he has given us and our God-given minds. Clearly, even though God is infinitely greater than our capacity for understanding, he wants us to try our best to understand him through his Word. And he has given us minds that are part of the image of God in us. The problem with appeal to mystery is that people give up trying to know and understand God too soon and use God's transcendence as an excuse not to think rightly about God. It is also a problem when people use God's holy otherness to criticize those who faithfully work to understand and explain God.

Let's talk about "mystery." A mystery is something *either* not yet revealed *or* revealed but beyond comprehension. If something has already been revealed and it is understandable, it is no longer a mystery. In Colossians 1:26–27 Paul refers to the "mystery that has been kept hidden for ages and generations, but is now disclosed to the Lord's people. To them God has chosen to make known among the Gentiles the glorious riches of this mystery, which is Christ in you, the hope of glory." Clearly, this is now no longer a mystery. It has been "made known." There may still be dimensions of it beyond complete comprehension, but Paul's use of "mystery" here is of a truth that was once unknown and is now known.

In Romans 11:32–36 Paul refers to a different kind of mystery—a truth that can only be uttered doxologically (in praise and worship) and that cannot be understood. "For God has bound everyone over to disobedience so that he may have mercy on them all." After all that Paul has said and that the Bible says about heaven and hell, what can this possibly mean? And why would God consign all people to disobedience? How can he have mercy on all when some clearly are headed to hell if not already there? Paul seems to realize he has reached the end of his powers of explanation. From there he simply goes into a song of praise to God's greatness:

Oh, the depth of the riches of the wisdom and knowledge
of God!
How unsearchable his judgments,
and his paths beyond tracing out!
"Who has known the mind of the Lord?
Or who has been his counselor?"
"Who has ever given to God,
that God should repay them?"
For from him and through him and to him are all things.
To him be glory forever! Amen.

Notice that Paul ends with appeal to mystery, but the inscruta-
bility of God's ways does not deter him from doing his best (with
the help of the inspiring Holy Spirit) to explain as much as the
mind can grasp. But it is as if he closes that great discussion of
God's sovereignty by saying, "Who can understand these things?
Praise be to God!" Too many folk Christians say something like that
before even trying to understand "these things" (i.e., the gospel
and God's will and ways).

In other words, "It's just a mystery" can mean one of two things.
Either, "It's difficult to understand so I'm not even going to try and
I wish you wouldn't either because it bothers me," or, "When all is
said and done and we've tried our best to comprehend God's will
and ways using his Word and our minds, we have to end by admitting there are depths to all this we will never grasp in this life."
The latter was Paul's way and has been the approach of most great
Christian thinkers down through the ages. The former is the way of
folk Christianity and is all too common in contemporary churches
and even Christian colleges, universities, and seminaries.

BAD PARADOX

Now let's relate mystery to paradox and vice versa. I've said
that there are appropriate and inappropriate appeals to mystery
in Christianity. I've said the same about paradox. Both are inappropriate when used as excuses for intellectual laziness or anti-

intellectualism. But now I must say that I am more comfortable with mystery than with paradox. Some wonderful Christian thinkers will disagree with me and say that paradox is the sign of mystery; mystery is best expressed with paradox. Perhaps. But I believe contradiction is always a sign of error; theological discourse is no exception.

I'll explain why more fully later. But for now, it is my conviction that logic, including the law of noncontradiction, is fundamental to communication including what goes on in my own mind. Insofar as I affirm two ideas that stand in absolute contradiction with each other, I have more work to do. Thankfully that's true in law. If a prosecutor presents a case against a defendant that contains contradictions, the jury is justified in acquitting the defendant. We do not think highly of people who contradict themselves. American philosopher and essayist Ralph Waldo Emerson said that foolish consistency is the hobgoblin of little minds. I disagree and so do most philosophers. Consistency is never foolish. It is the essence of integrity. How can we value integrity and denigrate consistency?

And yet, I agree that our thinking about God sometimes leads into paradoxes that are apparent contradictions. I suspect this will always be the case because of God's transcendence and our finitude and fallenness. I wonder, however, how much difference there really is between a real contradiction and an apparent contradiction? Only this—the hope that a contradiction can be resolved makes it a paradox. Insofar as I embrace and rest comfortably with a paradox, I am sacrificing my intellect and raising questions about my integrity. A lie is something that goes against truth. In a contradiction two things are affirmed as true when only one can really be true. If I affirm a contradiction, how am I not lying? Well, the intention may be different. And most people who affirm paradoxes have no consciousness of deceiving themselves or anyone. But objectively, quite apart from intention, isn't a paradox affirmed comfortably the same as an accepted contradiction and therefore a form of deceit about reality?

Maybe it would help if I give an example. (Some folks are going to be offended by any example I give, so I apologize in advance!) Some Christians desperately want to affirm two things they know seem to contradict each other—libertarian free will (including personal responsibility) and divine determinism. In other words, they want to have their cake and eat it too. Usually that's because they believe both are taught in the Bible. But inquiring minds will naturally want to know how these are compatible. How can a single act be determined by God and at the same time be the free and responsible choice of a creature? Call it paradox or antinomy (just another word for paradox) or whatever, it's still a problem.

Think about it. How can I be free and responsible when I commit a sin (and therefore am condemned to hell unless I repent and trust in Christ) and at the same time be determined by God (or anything outside myself) to commit that sin? Even some Calvinists shudder at that. They will say God never determines anyone to sin. Okay. What about Adam and Eve? Was their fall into sin foreordained by God? (I'm not talking about foreknowledge right now, just foreordination, which means a kind of predetermination.) John Calvin definitely affirmed it. So have many Calvinists. How could Adam and Eve have sinned freely if God rendered it certain? Appeal to Satan as a secondary cause does not solve the problem. If God predetermined it using any means or chain of causes, it does not seem that it could have been really free.

Most Calvinists recognize the problem and use a device called "compatibilism" to solve it. I respect that. It's an attempt (whether I agree that it works or not) to avoid sheer contradiction. Compatibilism is the idea that "freedom of choice" is compatible with determinism because we are "free" whenever we do what we want to do even if we could not do otherwise. Thus, Adam and Eve sinned "freely," even though God rendered it certain, because they wanted to sin. They would have been "unfree" only if someone had forced them to sin against their wills. This goes some way toward relieving the paradox, but it raises another set of questions, such as who instilled their desire to sin in them? How could God have foreordained and rendered their sin certain without somehow causing them to want to sin (even if through secondary causes such as Satan and their environment, etc.)? My point, though, is that at least these Calvinists are trying to use their God-given minds to avoid contradiction. It's better than those Christians who simply affirm two things that stand in black-and-white contradiction as equally true.

So what's bad about affirming contradiction? Why be so hard on people who do that? First, it makes it impossible to understand what they are saying. If someone comes up to you and says, "The sky is blue but it's not blue," that doesn't communicate anything; it only invites a question. If someone says, "I really love you but I really hate you," your understandable response would be, "What are you talking about?" If someone says, "This man is guilty of a terrible crime but he is innocent of it," you are perfectly justified in saying, "Huh?"

Now, of course, each of these paradoxes can be relieved by further explanation. Perhaps the sky is blue but not now because clouds are obscuring it. Oh, that explains it. Now there's no contradiction. Perhaps the person really does love you but at the moment is so angry with you that feelings of hate are getting in the way of the love. That's difficult, but not a sheer contradiction. Perhaps the man is technically guilty of a crime but innocent because he was forced to commit it (like the poor man around whose neck a remote control bomb was attached and he was forced to rob a bank). But if the two truths are affirmed as stated above without further explanation, the statements are extremely problematic — so much so that nobody could make any sense of them.

So it is in Christian discourse. If someone says, "God is good but also evil," I have no idea what they are saying. They might as well be speaking in an unknown language. Similarly with someone who says, "God is one but three." Without further explanation it makes no sense at all. It communicates nothing. Surely we should do our best to make our Christian communications intelligible. Paradox obscures intelligibility.

PARADOX AND APOLOGETICS

There's another but related reason why appeal to paradox is a problem. Most Christian apologists (defenders of the faith) are interested in showing that competing belief systems are inferior, and one of the major ways of showing that is by demonstrating their inner contradictions. This is a frequent and time-honored strategy of apologetics known technically as "eristics." It lies halfway between "polemics" (denouncing other belief systems as false) and "dialectics" (engaging in constructive dialogue across belief system boundaries and often affirming different truths as somehow equally true). The process of eristics explores the inner contradictions within worldviews and belief systems and attempts to show how one is better than others by demonstrating its greater coherence.

Many Christian philosophers and apologists have used this method (whether they called it eristics or not) to point to the truth of Christianity. Other, competing belief systems contain impossible contradictions at their cores. For example, German Catholic theologian Hans Küng wrote a book entitled *Does God Exist? An Answer for Today* (Doubleday, 1980). It is a marvelous example of irenic eristics. There Küng gently and respectfully demonstrates the weaknesses of atheism. He does not simply denounce atheists as fools. (Maybe he thinks they are, but the book comes across as more respectful of sincere and reflective atheists than that.) Nor does he compromise with atheism by affirming (like some radical theologians) "Christian atheism" (the idea of some radical theologians in the 1960s that God "died" in the rise of modern, secular culture).

Rather, Küng points out a deep, inner contradiction in most atheists' lives. He argues that atheism is one reasonable choice that people can make about the existence of God. God's reality can neither be proven nor disproven. Atheists are permitted to deny God's existence and be reasonable people. Unless! Unless they are unwilling to be nihilists. Nihilism is denial of the meaningfulness of reality and embrace of absurdity. Küng points out that many psychologists say that basic to human mental and emotional health is "fundamental trust" in the meaningfulness of reality. An atheist has no basis for fundamental trust. Only God provides it. Denial of God is consistent with nihilism but not with fundamental trust. Most atheists try to combine a denial of God with fundamental trust. Küng deftly shows the contradiction.

The reason for bringing up Küng and his book is simply to illustrate why appeal to paradox is a problem. Suppose someone could show that Küng himself falls into contradiction. Wouldn't that take away most if not all of the force of his argument against atheism? Surely it would. Other Christian philosophers and theologians have attempted to show that Hinduism contains an inner contradiction between belief in the oneness of everything (monism) and the duality between good and evil that drives karma. (I'm not judging whether that is a good or true argument against Hinduism but only noting that it is the most frequent one raised against it by Christians.) It seems to me that a Christian who appeals to paradox within the Christian belief system is not permitted to point out contradictions within other belief systems as if they are evidence of the falseness of those belief systems or the superiority of Christianity's claim to truth. When Christians embrace paradox and refuse to think further toward relieving it, they are simply undermining Christian eristics and giving permission to all kinds of non-Christian belief systems to do the same with impunity.

RELIEVING PARADOXES OF FAITH

All this naturally leads to the question of the alleged paradoxes within Christian belief. Someone may have reached this point in exasperation thinking, "What about the Trinity?" or, "What about the humanity and divinity of Jesus Christ?" Aren't these paradoxes? I believe they are not. The early church fathers worked hard to explain how the Christian belief in the triunity of God is not illogical even if it does point to a mystery beyond full comprehension. But most folk Christians are blissfully unaware of what the doctrine of the Trinity really says. At the great Council of Constantinople, the second universal council of the early Christian church in 381, the Christian leaders gathered agreed that God is *one substance* (*ousia*) but *three persons* (*hypostases*). They did *not* say "one in three, three in one" and leave it at that. Nor did they say "one substance and three substances" or "one person and three persons." Those would be paradoxes if not contradictions.

Later Christian thinkers have gone to great lengths to show how oneness and multiplicity (e.g., threeness) are not incompatible. Augustine did this in his classical *De Trinitate* (*On the Trinity*). So did many other Christian theologians and philosophers down through the centuries. In the twentieth century a British theologian named Leonard Hodgson wrote *The Doctrine of the Trinity* (Scribners, 1944), in which he showed that nature is full of what he called "organic unities"—entities that combine oneness with multiplicity. He also showed that "unity" and "oneness" do not always mean strict mathematical unity as in the number one. Most organisms are unities made up of interdependent parts. So, the doctrine of the Trinity is not a paradox even if our human minds can never fully comprehend the inner workings of the Godhead (mystery).

The same can be said of the humanity and divinity of Jesus Christ. The doctrine is not that Jesus Christ was "God wearing human skin" or "100 percent God and 100 percent man." Rather, as the early church fathers pointed out and as all orthodox Christians have since affirmed, the mystery of the incarnation of God in humanity is expressed in the truth that Jesus Christ was in person the eternal Son of God taking on human nature so that his identity was that of one person of the Trinity while he possessed two distinct (but never separate) natures—divine and human. There's no contradiction in this even if it is a mystery. It's a mystery because we know of no other personal identity possessing two distinct natures, and we don't know exactly how the two natures interacted. But the doctrine involves no apparent contradiction. And fortunately the church fathers who carved it out did not appeal to mystery too soon! They worked hard at making this belief intelligible before admitting there are depths to it beyond our full comprehension (e.g., how the two natures interact with each other).

What about free will and divine sovereignty? Like many non-Calvinists I take a different route to relieving the paradox than compatibilism. I believe God gives free will

> **REFLECTIVE** Christianity will always sit uncomfortably with paradox and seek ways to relieve the apparent contradiction without doing violence to Scripture.

as a gift and rules over it without determining our free choices. As I will explain in chapter 2, "God is in charge but not in control." Adam and Eve sinned freely; God did not render their fall certain. They could have done otherwise because God gave them power of contrary choice. But God allowed their defection from his will (he could have stopped it) and was prepared to fit what they did into his plan for redemption. No one can ultimately thwart God even if he allows us to do things against his will. The paradox is relieved. Reflective Christianity will always sit uncomfortably with paradox and seek ways to relieve the apparent contradiction without doing violence to Scripture.

DISCUSSION QUESTIONS

1. What role has appeal to paradox played in your Christianity? Have you been told or considered paradox a good thing to be embraced? After reading the chapter, what do you think about paradox?

2. Do you agree that American culture is too pragmatic — that it focuses too much on problem-solving to the neglect of abstract reasoning and speculation about reality behind appearances? In what ways (other than those listed in this chapter) has the pragmatic American culture influenced the church? Are you aware of other cultures where

pragmatism is not so pervasive? How has that reflected on the church there?

3. When do you think appeal to mystery is justified? Why?

4. What do you think about compatibilism as a way of resolving the divine sovereignty versus human freedom paradox? Does it work for you? Why or why not?

5. Is it unfair for Christians to appeal to mystery and paradox and at the same time criticize atheists or people of other religious faiths for embracing contradictions? Why or why not?

6. Do you agree that reflective, mature Christianity will always sit uncomfortably with paradox? Why or why not?

CHAPTER 2

GOD IS IN CONTROL:
SO WHY IS THE WORLD SUCH A MESS?

Perhaps one of the most common sayings of folk Christianity is: "God is in control." The day after I wrote the first draft of this chapter I happened to see a car with a bumper sticker that read "Relax! God is in control!" Often this saying is accompanied by the additional phrase, "so this was God's will" (where "this" refers to some calamity). Now, some Christians have given the matter a lot of thought and decided that the Bible does teach and they do believe that God controls everything that happens down to the tiniest details, including sin, evil, and calamities. They are usually Calvinists—followers of the sixteenth-century Reformer John Calvin and his later interpreters such as American Puritan Jonathan Edwards. Such people, including some popular Christian writers and speakers (e.g., John Piper, R. C. Sproul) have their reasons for believing that God is in control and that everything that happens is in some sense God's will.

When I was teaching theology at a leading evangelical college, then U.S. Surgeon General C. Everett Koop spoke in chapel. Since he was a leading crusader against tobacco smoking and chewing, I thought he would talk about the importance of taking care of our bodies. But instead he spoke for forty minutes on the subject "God Killed My Son." I knew that Koop was a member of Tenth Presbyterian Church of Philadelphia — a leading conservative Calvinist congregation pastored by one of my own seminary professors (James Montgomery Boice, who has since died). Koop expressed classical Calvinism in its starkest form. He related how his college-age son was killed in a mountain climbing accident a few years earlier and said that only his belief that God took his son's life gave him any comfort. If God took his son's life, it wasn't really an accident but an event filled with meaning and purpose even if those are hidden for now.

Koop believed that his son's death, like every other event, was planned and rendered certain by God in order to contribute to some yet mysterious greater good that God is unfolding through world history. For Koop and others like him, "God is in control, so whatever happens is God's will" is not just a trite saying. It is no cliché. It is a necessary expression of a deeply held belief in God's providence as all-encompassing and meticulous. As Calvinist author R. C. Sproul likes to say to underscore the necessity of God's total control of all things for his sovereignty: "If there is one single molecule in this universe running around loose, totally free of God's sovereignty, then we have no guarantee that a single promise of God will ever be fulfilled.... Without sovereignty God cannot be God. If we reject divine sovereignty then we must embrace atheism" (*Chosen by God* [Tyndale, 1986], pp. 26 – 27).

QUESTIONING AN APPARENT CONTRADICTION

For most Christians who say "God is in control and therefore this calamity is God's will," it is a problematic statement. That's because of other things they believe. During my twenty-some years of teaching Christian college students (and now seminary students) most of those who expressed this sentiment were not Calvinists. They believe strongly in free will, and most of them believe that God is unconditionally good and a God of love for all people (and especially children!). They would reject unequivocally the Calvinist idea that God's ultimate purpose in creation is to glorify himself even at the expense of children's deaths in gas chambers and the eternal suffering of some prechosen people in hell. When asked about the Holocaust or the Asian tsunami (or the horrible aftermath of Hurricane Katrina, which hit the southern U.S. just days before I am writing this), most of them would not attribute them to God's causal activity. And yet, like Calvinists (and Muslims), they continue to say in the face of every awful thing that happens, "God willed it."

Why would a non-Calvinist, a person who believes in freedom of will and God's benevolence toward all people, want to say that everything that happens is God's will without qualification or equivocation? It seems that this might be just a leftover attitude from the days when many of their spiritual ancestors were Calvinists. When such people switched from belief in God's all-determining rule to belief in creaturely freedom and from belief in divine determinism to belief in God as benevolent parent, they failed to change their platitudes about the reason things go wrong in the world.

Such folk Christians should stop and ask themselves whether they believe the fall of Adam and Eve in the primeval garden that led to the horrors of human history was God's plan and whether God willed it to happen. They should examine whether they believe Hitler was raised up by God as a scourge against God's own people the Jews (and others). Did God foreordain the Holocaust and manipulate the wills of its perpetrators? What about the twisted child abuser who kidnaps, tortures, and kills an innocent child? Does God foreordain and render that certain, or is it against his will?

If your answers to those questions add up to the idea that God does *not* foreordain, render certain, or cause such horrible deeds, then perhaps you should consider ceasing to say "God is in control; this was his will" when confronted by a terrible evil or horrendous disaster. If God is good in any sense analogous to our best understandings of personal goodness, what sense does it make to say that he controls history in an unlimited and unqualified fashion? That would mean he controls sin and evil as well. Of course, if by "control" one only means that God limits and governs, then all Christians would probably say God controls history. Nothing can happen without God's permission; that's pretty clear from Scripture and Christian tradition. It would seem to be part and parcel of the very idea of God. But when most people say "God is in control" and "God willed it," they mean that whatever has happened, however calamitous and evil, has been foreordained, planned and willed by God. If they don't mean that, they should be a bit more cautious and say rather that God has allowed it to happen.

The next question, of course, is "Why?" Equally sincere and astute Christians can go in different directions in answering this question, but they should be prepared to say something. Perhaps God can't always prevent even innocent suffering because he has self-imposed rules that govern his relationship with fallen creation. What would happen to free will if God always interfered with its consequences? This would be a different world if God did not allow the fallen wills of humans to do their work.

There are various ways of answering why God allows something evil or calamitous to happen. We all know of good and loving parents who allow their growing up children to make mistakes so that they can learn from them; they feel that the only way to stop them would be to control them by taking away their responsible freedom. God may have covenanted to partner with his creatures in history under certain rules by which he cannot prevent everything bad that happens. Perhaps God has decided that in most circumstances the "rain" (whether needed or destructive) will fall on both the righteous and the unrighteous.

This week, a week after Hurricane Katrina destroyed most of New Orleans, many people are asking, "Why did God let this happen?" Some Christians are saying, "It was God's will; trust God because he is always in control." That doesn't exactly sit well with most people who, for good biblical reasons, have trouble picturing the God of Jesus Christ wreaking death and destruction on children and families. A few people are daring to say, "God never intended people to build cities near oceans below sea level; that's our ancestors' doing and ours for living there." It may sound like blaming the victims, but in fact it is simply accepting our corporate responsibility for the evil in the world. Much, if not all, destruction of all kinds could be prevented if people lived lives of good common sense according to God's revealed will and were not ruled by selfish passion and pride.

> **MUCH,** if not all, destruction of all kinds could be prevented if people lived lives of good common sense according to God's revealed will and were not ruled by selfish passion and pride.

A similar case can be made about HIV/AIDS (and many diseases). God revealed his will about human sexuality, and it is against sexual promiscuity. While many people living with and dying of AIDS never engaged in promiscuous sex (or any sex for that matter!), experts are quite sure the virus entered into humanity via sexual perversion and promiscuity. Is AIDS, then, a judgment from God? Not exactly. But only folk religion answers that tough question with a knee-jerk and unequivocal "Yes!" or "No!" Why did God lay down laws for all humankind to live by? (I'm not here asking about laws only for Israel to keep its covenant with God.) Just to show who's in charge? Because God is a killjoy? Hardly. Perhaps God foresaw the consequences of sexual perversion and promiscuity and accordingly forbade them.

Why is there no mention of masturbation in the Bible? Could it be because God saw no particular harmful consequences arising from it? This is not to say that all masturbation is good or even neutral! Obsessive-compulsive sexual habits are something to avoid—they fall under the general heading of sexual perversion which in the New Testament is called *porneia* and is condemned.

GOD'S GOODNESS, POWER, AND THE PROBLEM OF EVIL

All this is simply to say that pat answers to difficult questions are seldom helpful. Simply to go around saying "It's God's will" in the face of every calamity, disease, accident, death, or war is to raise more questions. To go around saying "God is in control" is the same; it raises more questions than it answers. What kind of control does God exercise? How is it compatible with his goodness? What does "control" mean in a context of sin and evil and their consequences?

Once again, of course, if a person is truly a Calvinist and is prepared to explain and defend God's all-determining providential governance of all events, he or she has some warrant for saying these things. In that case they are not thoughtless platitudes that conflict with other beliefs. Nevertheless, even for the Calvinist further explanation is required. Does God will everything in the same way? Does God's all-encompassing control of history conflict with human responsibility? Are humans, then, mere robots? Why are people held responsible by God for doing what they are foreordained to do? What does God's goodness mean in a world where God plans and in some way (however indirectly) causes horrors like the Holocaust?

The Calvinist view of God's providence and power seems to lead into some thorny thickets of theological questioning. A Calvinist friend of mine wrote a book against a theological belief he considers nearly heretical. He declared that it diminishes God's glory and therefore is insulting and demeaning to God. I asked him whether he believes, as most Calvinists do, that God foreordains and renders certain everything for his glory. He affirmed it. Then

I asked him (quite honestly and with good intentions) how any belief, however heretical, can diminish God's glory if God foreordained it *for his glory*. See the problem? I still don't have an answer to that question.

In other words, even the Calvinist who declares that God is in control and that everything that happens is God's will needs to examine and explain further. People should not be faulted for asking tough questions about that. The father of Calvinism once brushed such objections and questions aside as little more than the barking of dogs. But is it really? Shouldn't he have taken the questions about God's goodness and human responsibility more seriously? I think he should have.

A basic rule of reflective Christianity is that you should strive to make your belief system biblical and coherent. In other words, if one of your beliefs conflicts with the Bible, you should certainly revise it. Unfortunately, it's not always easy to tell whether a belief conflicts with the Bible. The Bible is open to many interpretations. But there's another test of the truth of beliefs: consistency among them. If a person believes that God is benevolent, good, and loving and that human beings are responsible for what they do (under most circumstances) and liable to punishment for their acts, it makes little sense also to believe that God controls everything and that everything is according to God's will. Why? Because "everything" (unless further qualified) includes the first evil inclination in a creature's mind and heart (Satan's first rebellious thought in heaven before he fell and Adam's and Eve's first leanings toward sin) as well as all of the evil consequences that flow from that.

> A basic rule of reflective Christianity is that you should strive to make your belief system biblical and coherent.

Is God the author of sin and evil? Calvinists generally say no. But is that consistent with what they say about God's all-determining control? Non-Calvinists generally also deny that God is the author of sin and evil. But then why do they say "God is in control" and "Everything is God's will"? Such inconsistency cries out for resolution; the paradox needs relief. (In chapter 1 I discussed paradoxes and inconsistencies at some length.)

GOD IS IN CHARGE (EVEN IF NOT IN CONTROL)

Hopefully you will give careful thought to what you mean the next time you are tempted to say blithely, "God is in control." I have adopted a different way of expressing God's providential governance over history. I say, "God is in charge even though he doesn't control everything." It takes a few more words to say and it raises eyebrows. I'm then ready to explain what I mean. One student challenged my axiom and asked for further explication. I said "It's like this class; as the teacher I'm in charge, but clearly I'm not in control." The students laughed. They got the idea.

Of course, God is not exactly like a teacher and the world is not exactly like a classroom. But there may be an analogy. When I open a class at the beginning of the semester I have only good intentions for everyone and I do my best throughout the semester to help students achieve the goals and objectives of the course. I am interested in their well-being, including that they all get good grades. I try to run a fairly tight "ship," as it were, and keep the class sessions civil and organized. But much is also up to the students. Every teacher knows that students have a great deal of "say" in how a course evolves and how it ends up. No teacher in his or her right mind would try to manipulate the students; providing challenge and support is the most we should do.

What do students think of a teacher who begins the course by saying, "Because I grade on a curve it is predetermined that one fifth of you will fail"? Few students consider such a teacher benevolent. So, trying to be a good teacher, I do my best to remain "in charge" of the classroom and the entire course. I take responsibility for much of what happens. I guide and steer and prod and urge and offer all kinds of aids to learning. But at the end of the semester some students do poorly grade-wise. Whose fault is that? It would be my fault if I had not done my best to help them or if my expectations were simply unreasonably high. It would especially be my fault if I "controlled" the class and manipulated things so that some would fail.

Is it right to think of God along similar lines? Why not? I submit that most of the early church fathers (before Augustine) thought more or less this way. God is the creator and ruler of the universe, but he has given the terrible gift of moral freedom to human beings who have misused it. The world has spun out of God's control because he allowed it to happen. But he remains in charge. He has not abandoned his creation but seeks its redemption. Along the way many things happen that grieve God's heart and are against his will.

Perhaps we should make a distinction between God's antecedent will and God's consequent will. Before and apart from humanity's fall into sin no such distinction was necessary. Since sin entered the world, everything that happens is according to God's consequent will in that he allows it. The only alternative would be to abolish free will. God limits evil and steers the course of history along certain lines according to his covenant with people. But he does not cause everything either directly or indirectly. (Of course, nothing would exist without God's creative causation, but here we are talking about his causality of specific events.)

Some people object to my formula that God is in charge but not in control because they think it undermines his power. I disagree. God has the power to stop anything from happening; he just doesn't always exercise that power. God limits the exercise of his power for the sake of real, free relationships with people and for the sake of creatures' moral responsibility. (In this respect my teacher and class analogy breaks down; unlike God I am not omnipotent!)

> GOD limits the exercise of his power for the sake of real, free relationships with people and for the sake of creatures' moral responsibility.

Others object to my formula because they think it robs them of the comfort of believing that everything has a purpose. Perhaps they should become Calvinists (in which case they would have to live with another set of problems). I wonder what comfort they derive from believing that God controls everything. What comfort is in believing that God manipulates events so that children contract leukemia and die slow, agonizing deaths? What comfort comes with believing that Hitler was an instrument in the hands of God? Sure, these beliefs may invest meaning and purpose in such otherwise absurd events, but what do they say about God?

I don't find such a "hidden God" (as Luther called the side of God that wreaks havoc and evil on the world) comforting at all. Such a God is not revealed in Jesus Christ and is more like a terrible tyrant than a loving heavenly Father. If there is a "hidden God" as some believe and as at least one hymn proclaims ("Behind a frowning providence God hides a smiling face"), how can we trust God to be good? How can we believe in God's promises? Perhaps part of God's hiddenness is that he doesn't keep his promises. Once the "hidden God" idea is introduced, all kinds of questions pop up out of the Pandora's box it opens.

I prefer simply to say that God is in charge but not in control. It's less misleading, given everything that I believe, than "God is in control." I also prefer to say that some things happen against God's will; God does not always get his way. It's less problematic than "Everything is according to God's will." Of course, I add that God *could* be in control, but he chooses not to be. And I add that whatever happens is at least allowed by God.

If pushed to explain how allowing the Holocaust is better than foreordaining it, I appeal to common experience. There are many things I have to allow because to stop them would require violence beyond my moral ability to exercise. I have agreed to live within the social contract that says I cannot act as my own police force. I have to allow the duly appointed police to do their work. I cannot be a vigilante. As my daughters matured and entered adulthood, I had to let go of my attempts to control them. I had to let them make mistakes—even when I could have stopped them—so they could learn from them. So God restrains himself for a time so that human history can be what it is—an enterprise involving freedom and responsibility. (In chapter 5 we'll discuss how this idea of God's self-restraint and human freedom applies to the thorny problem of finding God's will for life.)

GOD IS NOT NICE

It is important that we critically examine another platitude often mouthed by well-meaning Christians, one that is just as much folk religious as "God is in control." It arises at the opposite end of the spectrum of folk beliefs about God and is often an overreaction to belief in God's all-determining control of history. More than a few times I've heard students and church people say about biblical narratives of God's wrath, "My God would never do that!" Another way this sentimental idea of God manifests is in response to questions about God's role in natural disasters including plagues, famines, and floods: "God would never do that."

Am I contradicting myself when I suggest that this also may be too facile? I don't think so. Although God is good, biblical revelation shows us that God's patience has its limits and that he does occasionally interfere in human history in terrible ways. I'm always a bit put off when people assert confidently that a certain calamity has nothing to do with God. Really? How can we know that?

True, we can be sure that God does not intend to harm innocents; he is not like some arbitrary tyrant who wipes out whole villages including children just because he's angry or because he wants to display his power and displeasure. But if God is going to pronounce his judgment against, say, a city or country, how could he do it without risking what is euphemistically known as "collateral damage"? What if a whole city became so horribly corrupt that even the children were living and dying in squalor and abuse and suffering day in and day out because of the adults' evil decisions and actions? Might it be merciful of God to wipe that city off the face of the earth? After all, God is God and not subject to the laws he has imposed on us. I, for example, am not allowed to shoot at a fleeing criminal. But a police officer is — under the right circumstances.

This offends many people's sensibilities about God. They're not the ones who say "God is in control." (I've already offended them!) They are the ones who have a sentimental notion of God as "nice." But where does the Bible say that God is nice? As C. S. Lewis said through one of the characters of the *Chronicles of Narnia* (about the lion, Aslan, who symbolizes Christ), God is good but not safe. So I say God is good but not nice. "Nice" is a human convention; it is a way we get along with each other and is completely compatible with indifference. I'm nice because that's what is expected of me. (Of course, I like to think I'm also just a nice person!) But as one of my former colleagues liked to say, "It's nice to be nice but it's better to be helpful."

Nice can be a way of putting people off; it can be a tool of manipulation or a means to avoid confrontation. I'm not saying nice is bad; in most circumstances it's okay. But it isn't a virtue. Kindness is a virtue, but that's not the same as niceness. Nice implies polite and can be superficial. Kind suggests a more sincere care and giving. Nice is incompatible with tough love; kind isn't. By all biblical accounts God is kind, but nothing in the Bible suggests that God is nice. God's kindness can be terrible as revealed in some of his Old Testament acts against the enemies of his people. Sometimes in order to be kind to one group of people I have to be tough toward another group. So it is with God.

We do God no favors by creating him in our own image. Someone quipped that God created humans in his image and ever since humans have been returning the favor. Too many folk Christians like to think that God is like a nice old grandfather who would never harm a flea. That may be sentimental and sweet, but it is hardly the biblical picture of God, who is often a warrior and a terrible avenger. The God of the Bible is longsuffering and shows loving-kindness, but only up to a point. I think it is right to believe that God is too great and good to lose his temper; losing one's temper is a trait of human frailty. So, when the biblical narratives reveal God wreaking vengeance on people by

WE do God no favors by creating him in our own image.

destroying cities and whole groups of people, we should not interpret that as God simply "losing it," so to speak. Rather, we should think that God has good reasons for destroying people when he does that. Frankly and put bluntly, they needed destroying. In Texas there's a common response when certain kinds of people are killed (such as a child or wife abuser): "He needed killin'."

Our modern sensibilities go against thinking that God kills people. But if we take the Bible seriously, it's hard to avoid. We have to suppose they "needed killin'," as harsh as that sounds. But can we ever know today what God is doing or how God is involved (if at all) in a natural disaster? I don't think so. But we shouldn't make flat-out claims such as "God didn't have anything to do with that" or "My God wouldn't do something like that." How can we know that? We can be sure that God does not cause people to sin, but we can't be sure that God does not himself occasionally reach the end of his patience and send a hurricane or an earthquake.

> WE should be careful about making blanket statements about what God does or does not do.

After all, much of the Bible indicates he will do that at the end of history! What warrant do we have for saying confidently he doesn't do it before then? We should be careful about making blanket statements about what God does or does not do. Some things we can rule out (or in) based on his own self-revelation and the character we know him to have because of that revelation. But we have no grounds for saying that God would never cause the calamity that befalls a city or country.

EXAMINING BELIEFS ABOUT GOD

The point of this chapter, as of the whole book, is to encourage Christians to stop and examine their platitudes and clichés as well as the beliefs that underlie them. Too often they are not based on any thought processes and are unexamined. They are borrowed from others because they sound good. Perhaps they bring some level of comfort. But too often they raise more questions than they answer and plant ideas about God in people's minds that are confusing, inconsistent, unbiblical, or even dishonoring to God.

I'm not arguing that it is always wrong to say "God is in control," or "This is God's will." I am arguing that if we say that, we should be prepared to explain and qualify. Perhaps we should always offer such qualifications and explanations knowing that such simple sayings raise questions our hearers may not have the courage to ask. But I have found it better to say "God is in charge but not in control," and "God allows whatever happens but not everything is according to his perfect will." Adding just a few words makes a world of difference. Even then, however, I often find it necessary to go on to explain and defend in order to avoid confusion and offense.

Reflective Christianity means I can't even settle comfortably with these nuanced statements about God. After all, as emphasized in the introduction, no theology or system of belief is ever absolutely correct and complete. But for now, I find these expressions better than alternatives with which I am familiar. Yet I remain open to correction; I continue to examine whether there might be better ways of expressing God's involvement in world history and people's lives. I don't think there is a perfect, permanent Christian language. Our ways of expressing faith in God and explaining his ways will continue to evolve as we strive for deeper understanding. Maybe ten years from now my own study of Scripture together with my own life experiences and my rational thought processes will lead me to revise my preferred way of expressing these things. I remain open to that. What I am confident will never change is my faith in God's goodness.

DISCUSSION QUESTIONS

1. Do you consider yourself a Calvinist or inclined that way? If so, what is your belief about God's sovereign control over history? If not, what is your belief about it? (What default viewpoint tends to govern your approach to this subject?)

2. When have you heard people say "God is in control," and "This was God's will"? What events provoked those kinds of sentiments? Having read this chapter, how would you evaluate the appropriateness of these statements to the events?

3. Do you think AIDS is God's judgment? In what sense? Did you have an emotional reaction to the section on God and AIDS? If so, what was it?

4. What kind of response do you have (initially and perhaps after some thought) to the formula "God is in charge but not in control"? Does it help you think more clearly about God's providence, or does it seem to detract too much from God's majesty?

5. Before reading this chapter did you tend to think of God as "nice"? How did that translate into your view of God and events in the world? After reading the chapter what do you think about God's "niceness"?

6. What are some other unexamined beliefs about God besides those discussed in this chapter? What do you think about them now? What might you say to a person who spouts unexamined or simplistic clichés about God such as those?

CHAPTER 3

JESUS IS THE ANSWER:
SO WHAT'S THE QUESTION?

There's an old joke among evangelicals and perhaps especially among Baptists. It's about one Sunday school boy advising another, younger Sunday school boy how to answer the teacher's questions: "The answer is always Jesus." I can't count how many times I've heard this said facetiously even by my college and seminary students as they discussed together what the right answers are to the questions that might be on the test. "The answer is always Jesus." Of course, the joke means that in Sunday school you're always safe saying "Jesus" even if that's not the right answer!

This correlates well with the now fairly old evangelical slogan "Jesus is the answer!" You see it on bumper stickers, on Christian jewelry (and other "holy hardware" sold in Christian "bookstores"), and on bus stop benches and even billboards. It seems to have risen to prominence during the Jesus People movement of the late 1960s and early 1970s when Jesus People chanted "Jesus! Jesus! Jesus!" repeatedly at large rallies and small coffeehouse gatherings. Around that time a popular Christian song carried the slogan into its chorus: "Jesus is the answer for the world today...."

Every evangelical Christian in America knows this slogan: "Jesus is the answer." Many non-Christians know it too—often to their chagrin or amusement. Some wag long ago circulated the response, "So, what's the question?" That's about as trite as the slogan itself! (So I apologize for using it in the title of this chapter!) However, it raises an important reminder to folk Christians and others about the pluralistic culture in which we live and try to evangelize.

It's pretty standard now for seminary professors to teach prospective missionaries how to read and interpret the culture into which they move in order to contextualize the gospel message. The gospel needs to be translated into the cultural idiom if it is to be understood. We've all heard of the American missionaries who took their American cultural baggage with them to foreign mission fields and attempted to impose a distinctly American form of Christianity on the "natives," with little or no sensitivity to their cultural customs. But has the lesson of contextualizing the gospel message sunk in about evangelizing people in America? For better or for worse, America is a tremendously diverse and pluralistic culture. Especially in the larger cities of the Northeast, Upper Midwest, and Western regions (just about everywhere except the Deep South!), one can no longer assume that people even have a clue what you mean when you declare that "Jesus is the answer!"

PROBLEMS WITH "JESUS IS THE ANSWER"

The simple declaration that "Jesus is the answer!" unaccompanied by any further explanation is evidence of folk Christianity for two reasons. First, it raises the question, "What are the questions?" and assumes that people can and will understand what the questions are and how Jesus is their answer. Many people in today's American culture (and other cultures) have no clue what the intended question or questions might be or how Jesus constitutes their answer. Outside the Bible Belt we can no longer assume that most people have even a passing familiarity with Jesus or the way in which he is the answer to certain important questions.

Second, "Jesus is the answer!" is folk religion insofar as it promotes what some scholars have called a functional unitarianism of the second person of the Trinity. German Catholic theologian Karl Rahner argued in his little book entitled simply *The Trinity* (Seabury Press, 1974) that most Christians are functionally unitarians in that they focus attention exclusively on Jesus and ignore the Father and Holy Spirit.

Who can deny that about folk evangelicalism? Most evangelicals know little (and perhaps care less!) about the great Christian doctrine of the Trinity, and in their near obsession with Jesus they forget the other two persons of the Godhead. While "Jesus is the answer!" is not entirely wrong, it lacks depth; it falls short of connecting with most people in today's secular and pagan culture who can't even understand it, and it falls short of expressing the historic Christian claim that the Trinity is the answer. "The Trinity is the answer"? It just doesn't have the same ring as "Jesus is the answer!" does it? Nope. But since when do Christians care about what has the Madison Avenue ring? We should care more about truth than effectiveness.

Far be it from me to denigrate Jesus or remove him from his well-deserved special place in evangelical religious life. All my life I've worshiped him and prayed to him and participated eagerly in Jesus-centered evangelicalism. I love Jesus. But I also realize that popular evangelicalism has a tendency to be so focused on Jesus that it loses touch with the historic and biblical truth about the fullness of the trinitarian Godhead of God.

First, then, "Jesus is the answer!" (whether with or without the exclamation mark) falls short of speaking meaningfully to many people because of contemporary culture's pluralism. Too many Christians, especially young Christians, are sheltered by their evangelical subculture from the fact that many people in the world around them have no idea who Jesus is or what questions he is supposed to answer.

> POPULAR evangelicalism has a tendency to be so focused on Jesus that it loses touch with the historic and biblical truth about the fullness of the trinitarian Godhead of God.

Often they've been home schooled or have surrounded themselves with only Christian friends at public schools. If they grew up in the Bible belt of America, they probably fail to realize how culturally different other parts of the country are. Many Bible belt churches take their youth groups on "mission trips" to large American cities in the North or Midwest or on the Pacific Coast. There the well-intentioned young evangelists go around proclaiming "Jesus is the answer!" and wonder at the icy stares they receive from passing crowds. Are they hostile or what? Well, maybe they don't have a clue what you mean!

My family and I sadly observed this when we lived in Germany in the early 1980s. Many centers of large German (and other European) cities are gathering places for all kinds of people, and American church and parachurch youth groups tended to focus their attention there by putting on skits and singing and witnessing among the crowds. We occasionally stood back among the Germans (and tourists) and watched and listened as young people of our own American religious subculture tried to connect with the Europeans among whom we lived. The experience was a real eye-opener for us. Often the well-intentioned, clean-cut young American evangelists spouted American evangelical clichés such as "Jesus is the answer!" without realizing what we knew from living "on the economy" (i.e., not on an American military base).

Most German city dwellers are thoroughly secular. They never think of Jesus except perhaps as a relic of Germany's religious past. Crucifixes are everywhere, especially in Bavaria, the southernmost part of the country. But even there hardly anyone thinks of Jesus except as the God of the medieval religion that once dominated their culture. We wished that the fervent young missionaries knew what we knew about our neighbors. Perhaps in that case they would make more of an effort to contextualize their message for their thoroughly secular audience.

The point here is that this very secularity or at least philosophical, religious, and spiritual pluralism exists in America. Most Americans are well aware of evangelical Christianity, although many equate it with one segment—the so-called "religious right." Most know who Jesus was and are aware that at least conservative Christians still worship him as God. But one can no longer assume any knowledge beyond that. Especially in urban areas you now see Buddhist temples sitting in the suburbs among the Cape Cod style houses with their picket fences. Atheists are organized and sit on school boards and run for public office on a subtle platform of opposing religious influence in society. Many people who grew up Christian now follow Eastern religions and practice Transcendental Meditation or are attracted to Scientology or any number of other new religious movements that have little or nothing to do with Christianity. In certain trendy urban areas (often called "Uptown"), public mention of Jesus will raise thoughts of David Koresh and the Branch Davidians or fears of the religious right and its perceived threat to individual freedoms. Immigration from Asian countries and from Africa and the Middle East has swelled the ranks of those with no Christian background who may have heard of Jesus but have no clue what "Jesus is the answer" means.

DISCERNING THE CULTURAL CONTEXT

The problem is not just with this single platitude, of course. It is with many folk Christians' ignorance of the contemporary, post-Christian (and perhaps even post-religious) context of American culture. They expect people to understand what some scholars have called "the language of Zion" (distinctively traditional Christian

God-talk) when many have no way of understanding it. Not only is "Jesus is the answer" incomplete for them; it is simply unintelligible. So are other folk Christian evangelistic "hooks" used to draw people into conversation if not conversion.

So am I saying that Christians should simply abandon "Jesus is the answer" and similar clichés? Not necessarily. What I am arguing is that we should surround them with cultural sensitivity, which often means some kind of explanation. People need to know to what questions Jesus is the answer. We can no longer assume that everybody has the same burning question to which they will immediately recognize Jesus as the answer.

The German Protestant theologian Dietrich Bonhoeffer, who was killed by the Nazis in 1945 for involvement in a plot to assassinate Hitler, wrote about this problem in his *Letters and Papers from Prison*, which were published posthumously. There he recommended something he called "religionless Christianity." Scholars have debated ever since what he meant. But I don't think it's all that opaque. Bonhoeffer was an astute student of culture and a prophetic voice. He saw where Western culture was going—toward a kind of radical secularity in which no single religious vision of life could be taken for granted. He asked what Christianity would have to be like in such a world where Christians could no longer assume a "religious a priori"—a spiritual point of contact for the gospel—in every human heart. What would happen to Christianity in a society where people no longer sense the need of God in order to live happy and fulfilled lives? What if the day comes when most people don't even feel guilty for being sinful but instead wrestle with other problems such as self-esteem, success, and relationships? What if people no longer identify with Martin Luther, who searched for a merciful God?

Most evangelical Christians simply assume that (in the words of another cliché) everybody has a "God-shaped empty place" in their heart. This is a popular expression of ancient church father Augustine's statement that God made people restless until they found their rest in God. Bonhoeffer was envisioning a day when that perspective would no longer be true or could not be assumed. What if people are perfectly content with their lives or with whatever philosophical or religious answers they have found and sense no need of the gospel or Jesus Christ?

Bonhoeffer's musings in some of his letters from prison upset a lot of people—especially those who believe that underneath the secular or pagan exterior all people secretly know their need of God but simply live in denial. C. S. Lewis believed that. While he never addressed Bonhoeffer's questions (so far as I know), he did argue in *Mere Christianity* that there is a "law of nature" that includes an inward sense of right and wrong and of being in the wrong. People know, whether they admit even to themselves or not, that they are accountable to someone greater than themselves and that they do not measure up to transcendent standards of who they are supposed to be. But whether people secretly know this or not, Bonhoeffer's point seems to stand that many people in contemporary society do not seem to connect with traditional Christian messages that tell them God or Jesus is the answer to their most important questions.

MAKING THE CONNECTION WITH THE AUDIENCE

So what is the answer to contextualizing the Christian message in our increasingly pluralistic culture with its growing populations of secular and pagan people? Reflective Christianity knows there is no simple answer. With Bonhoeffer we realize that we cannot grab people by their intellectual lapels and argue them into accepting Jesus by (as Bonhoeffer put it) pouncing on their weakness and insisting that they can only find fulfillment in him. A lot of them simply won't know what we are talking about. But with Lewis I affirm that every mature human person knows in his or her subconsciousness that life is empty without a transcendent source, foundation, and goal. While there may not be a "God-shaped empty place" in every human heart and while people may not be aware of being restless until they find rest in God, I believe everyone has an awareness of something lacking apart from connection with an eternal love.

That's the way I would put it today. People may not wrestle with finding a merciful God the way Luther did. They may not be riddled with guilt as he was. They may not be aware of any need that God or Jesus could fill. But in their deepest moments of solitude, intimations of God seep in through feelings of loneliness that no earthly friendship can satisfy and through longings for acceptance, acknowledgment, and love that no worldly relationship can fulfill.

> **WHILE** there may not be a "God-shaped empty place" in every human heart and while people may not be aware of being restless until they find rest in God, I believe everyone has an awareness of something lacking apart from connection with an eternal love.

Folk religion blithely tosses spiritual clichés at people as if they can understand them. It wrongly assumes that everyone is somewhere on the same playing field and that they all can understand the same signals. It fails to grasp the problem of cultural differences. The Christian language game can no longer be assumed; many people in contemporary America don't know the rules. Simply to say "Jesus is the answer" or "I found it" (the slogan of a 1970s-era evangelistic campaign) or similar sweet platitudes falls short of connecting with people we want to accept Jesus.

When Paul went to Athens (Acts 17), he didn't plunge immediately into a string of clichés but sought out the place where the religious seekers gathered and looked for a point of contact. There he found an altar to the "unknown god," and he began with that. Eventually he worked his way to Jesus, but not before sensitively establishing common ground with his listeners. Reflective Christianity is aware of the limitations of Christian language in today's public square. And it knows that the common ground between the gospel and especially Christian theology and many contemporary people is difficult to find. I believe it is there in our common humanity, but I never assume I know exactly what it is until I'm in a situation of communication with a non-Christian. Reflective Christianity is wary of one-size-fits-all evangelism and respects non-Christians' differences of worldview, culture, and personality.

So is "Jesus is the answer" all wrong? Of course not. Like every folk Christian slogan, it contains some truth. Among Christians, certainly, it is safe to say. We know what it means. We've found the answer to our deepest questions about forgiveness, acceptance, and eternal love in him. It's probably not a helpful answer to even open-minded spiritual seekers we encounter in the marketplace of contemporary culture. It is less appealing as a conversation starter unless we are willing and able immediately to explain what questions Jesus answers. Even then we should be prepared for our questions to be different from those of our conversation partners.

"Jesus is the answer" to everyone's deepest, often unconscious questions — questions they probably cannot even articulate. Rather than tossing out "Jesus is the answer," why not begin with friendly conversation about music, popular culture, personal aims and goals, relationships, and problems of the world? Let the Spirit of God steer the conversation into paths that open up possibilities for witness through sharing your story of how you found answers to your deepest questions and needs in Jesus Christ and in having a relationship with him? Trust that somewhere deep down in your conversation partner's existence is an ultimate need — the question to which Jesus *is* the answer. It may be the need for an eternal friend who accepts and loves unconditionally. Or it may be the need for hope for a better world. Or it may be the need for forgiveness when people whom the person has wronged are not willing or able to forgive. Only when the proper need to which Jesus really is the answer arises should you say "Jesus is the answer," and then be ready to explain how that is so.

THE TRINITY IS THE ANSWER?

There's another dimension of "Jesus is the answer" (and similar sayings about Jesus) that we need to look at critically. Is Jesus alone really the answer? Where do we get the idea that Jesus is all of God wrapped up in a man? Admittedly some New Testament passages (e.g., Colossians 1:19) seem to say something like this. And some Christians have adopted a "Jesus Only" theology in which the whole Godhead—Father, Son, and Holy Spirit—is subsumed under the identity of Jesus Christ. (This theology is widespread among some Pentecostals and was known as modalism or Sabellianism in the early Christian churches. Today it often goes under the label of "Oneness theology.")

Many other evangelical Christians simply unthinkingly ignore or neglect the other two persons of God and focus exclusively on Jesus. Such a functional unitarianism of the second person of the Trinity is widespread in evangelical and perhaps other Christian circles. After all, Jesus is God incarnate and God is one God and Jesus is God with a human face, so we can identify with him and have a personal relationship with him. It's a little hard to picture the Holy Spirit or the Father.

Far be it from me to knock Jesus piety. I grew up with it and still live in it most of the time. Jesus was a living, almost palpable if invisible presence in the home and church of my childhood. My parents walked and talked with him all the time. Especially my stepmother carried on a seemingly continuous conversation with Jesus as if he were right there standing at the kitchen sink with her. She believed he was. At church we sang songs about Jesus and prayed to him, and there was a huge picture of Jesus praying in the garden of Gethsemane painted on the wall (floor to ceiling!) behind the pulpit. Somewhere I learned that there was also the Father (the person Jesus was praying to!) and the Holy Spirit (we were Pentecostals), but very little was said about them. I was never encouraged to develop a relationship with them or even think about them or the entire Godhead. Along the way in my spiritual journey I learned about the Trinity (probably in a pretty distorted fashion), but to me it was sort of a relic of ancient Christianity that didn't live except in some hymns we occasionally sang.

I suspect that's a common experience of growing up in the American evangelical subculture. But at some point in my journey toward reflective Christianity I came to know of the church fathers, who suffered much to keep the persons of the Trinity distinct but all equally God. I learned to admire Athanasius, the great Egyptian Christian leader of the fourth century, who stood virtually alone against emperors who sought to impose a non-Trinitarian version of Christianity on everyone. I studied under an Eastern Orthodox theologian who extolled the Trinity as a community of divine persons who takes us up into that community of love as we yield our lives to God's deifying power. ("Deification" is an Eastern Orthodox expression of the New Testament idea that God shares something of his divine nature with us in salvation; see 2 Peter 1:4.) I read books by ancient, medieval, Reformation, and modern Christians who underscored the importance of the Trinity for Christian worship, spirituality, and everyday living. Gradually I began to realize that the Christianity of my childhood and youth was missing something—attention to the Father and the Holy Spirit as persons in their own right alongside the Son, Jesus Christ.

One book that helped me grasp the fullness of the Godhead and grow out of my Jesusology was *The Forgotten Father* (Wipf & Stock, 2001) by British evangelical theologian Thomas Smail. *I Believe in the Holy Spirit* (Eerdmans, 2004) by British charismatic theologian Michael Green brought more clearly to my mind and heart the personal nature of the Spirit. Neither of these books neglected Jesus. He is the revelation of the Father and the giver of the Holy Spirit, who, in turn, seeks to glorify Jesus. But both books (and others) helped me rediscover the broader Christian teaching about the whole Trinity; they led me to a catholic evangelical faith that connects with the great tradition of Christian teaching about God as three distinct persons sharing one eternal substance equally.

All three persons are important to a holistic Christian faith and life. I have never left behind my love for and special relationship with Jesus. Even as a fifty-something-year-old theologian I still consider myself (as in the 1970s) a "Jesus freak"! I pray to Jesus and talk about him, and when I have to select a new church to join (because of a move) I always look for one that is Jesus-centered.

I object to replacing talk of Jesus with vague, generic talk of "God" ("Gaawwwd!"). But I've learned to add the entire Trinity to my spiritual life or, perhaps better put, to dwell spiritually with the whole Trinity and not just one person.

A problem with "Jesus is the answer" is that it can reinforce a common evangelical reduction of the Trinity to one person—- Jesus. Of course, that one cliché is not to blame by itself! Evangelical Christianity has inherited its functional unitarianism of the second person of the Trinity from some of the early Pietists, such as German Count Nikolaus Ludwig von Zinzendorf, the leader of the Moravian community. By all accounts he was obsessed with Jesus to the neglect of the Father and the Spirit. One modern scholar described the German count as "the noble Jesus freak." Zinzendorf deeply impacted the entire evangelical movement from his time in the early eighteenth century on. Revivalism has played a role in the common evangelical exclusive focus on Jesus; Billy Graham (like earlier mass revivalists) has always talked about Jesus with a special emphasis ("Jeeesssuuusss!"), sometimes mocked by imitators.

I respect Billy Graham and Zinzendorf and the whole line of evangelists between them. But I also think we evangelicals are missing something insofar as we neglect the Trinity. Jesus is part of God, not the whole of God. (This isn't really a very felicitous way of putting it; the Trinity cannot be divided into parts! But how else do you make this point? I have to say this for other theologians who are reading this book.) Trinitarian life, as I learned from my Eastern Orthodox teacher and from friends, is more than just Jesus piety. Knowing Jesus and communing with him is essential for authentic evangelicalism, and we evangelicals can teach our more staid and traditional Christian brothers and sisters about that. But they can teach us that knowing and communing with Jesus is one dimension, however crucial, within a larger spiritual-

> I'VE learned to add the entire Trinity to my spiritual life or, perhaps better put, to dwell spiritually with the whole Trinity and not just one person.

ity of being taken up into the life of the Trinity and enjoying the fellowship between Father, Son, and Holy Spirit.

So what can we learn about reflective Christianity from a critical look at the slogan "Jesus is the answer"? I hope nobody comes to the end of the chapter thinking I am against Jesus or opposed to saying that he is the answer. But, like other popular clichés, such as the ever-present "What Would Jesus Do?" ("WWJD?"), it has its limitations and can do more harm than good unless it is wrapped in proper understanding and offered with sensitivity and further explanation. Left as it is, without clarification, it can be misleading and needlessly offensive.

> **KNOWING** and communing with Jesus is one dimension, however crucial, within a larger spirituality of being taken up into the life of the Trinity and enjoying the fellowship between Father, Son, and Holy Spirit.

People in popular culture (movies, music, literature, television shows, comedy) have picked it up and used it as a point of ridicule against evangelical Christians. Could that be because it has been trivialized by being thrown out into the public square of culture without reflective wrapping? As it stands, it is just too naked to be helpful in most situations. It sounds trite and even stupid insofar as it simply does raise the question, "What's the question?" Most inquiring minds will regard it as a ploy to force open conversation into which evangelical Christianity can be triumphalistically inserted.

Furthermore, it ignores the fullness of the Godhead when it is used so often and so freely. Yes, Jesus is the answer in that he alone died on the cross for our sins and rose from the dead to give us new life. But the Father was there behind the cross sacrificing his only Son, and the Holy Spirit was raising him from the dead and energizing the church into a world-transforming force. Reflective Christianity does not reject such a well-intentioned slogan as "Jesus is the answer" in knee-jerk fashion. But it uses it cautiously and appropriately and balances it with sensitivity to culture and to the classic Christian idea of the Trinity.

DISCUSSION QUESTIONS

1. Have you ever witnessed or overheard Christians being insensitive to their cultural context? What are some other examples besides ones discussed in this chapter?

2. Do you agree that popular, folk evangelicalism tends to focus too much on Jesus to the neglect of the other persons of the Godhead? If so, what are some ways to arrive at a more balanced theology and worship and do justice to the whole Trinity?

3. What do you think of Bonhoeffer's "religionless Christianity"? Does that phrase have a negative ring to you? Or does it provoke a positive response? Why? What might "religionless Christianity" look like in your social location?

4. What do you think about the popular question "What would Jesus do?" (WWJD?)? What are some problems with that as a guide to ethical conduct?

5. Do you recognize modalism (Sabellianism) as part of what you were taught about the Trinity or how you have come to think about it? What are the errors of this view? How do you think of the Trinity now? How would you respond to someone who espouses modalistic theology?

6. As a result of reading this chapter do you feel you have a better grasp of the Christian doctrine of the Trinity? What unresolved questions do you still have about it? Where might you look for answers?

CHAPTER 4

THE BIBLE HAS ALL THE ANSWERS:

SO WHAT ABOUT CLONING?

Evangelical folk Christianity abounds with myths about the Bible. One book published several years ago carried the title *That Manuscript from Heaven*. The cover displayed the planets, sun and other stars, and the moon above with the earth's surface below. Between was an open Bible descending as if from "heaven" down to earth. The impression created by the cover, including the title, was that the entire Bible simply fell out of heaven.

I grew up in a tiny denomination that reverenced the Bible. In fact, it had the word "Bible" in its name. At home I was not allowed to place anything on top of a Bible, including my Sunday school quarterly. (Only people around my age and older will probably remember what a "Sunday school quarterly" was.) Overall I gained the impression from my parents (especially my stepmother) and others in our church that the Bible shares in God's own divine nature. It certainly was to us like a blessed icon is to Eastern Orthodox or Roman Catholics.

Over the years I've heard countless well-meaning evangelical Christians extol the virtues of the Bible as a collection of blessed promises and answers to life's questions. Want the answer to anything? It's in the Bible. Of course they didn't mean to turn there to find what brand of refrigerator to buy! For the most part, anyway, even the least sophisticated evangelical Christian knows that the Bible's answers are religious and ethical in nature. (Although I've met a few who seem to think you can magically find the answer to virtually any important question in the Bible by asking God to lead you directly to a verse that will point toward the right answer.) For many folk Christians the Bible is all you need when it comes to finding the solutions to life's ultimate questions, including thorny issues of contemporary politics, ethics, and moral decision making.

The corresponding popular platitude is "The Bible has the answer." Sometimes it is expressed in other ways, such as "Look in the book." Even where no particular cliché expresses the attitude, it may yet exist. Especially fundamentalist (the most conservative of the conservative) Christians tend to treat the Bible as if every subject one might study in school arises out of the Bible—or at least every subject ought to be taught with the Bible in its background, helping to guide us away from some contemporary answers toward others.

FOLK RELIGION AND THE BIBLE

I attended a fundamentalist Bible college. The first year the board of regents appointed a man to be its president who I now realize was deeply into folk Christianity. He insisted that the Bible be the center of the school's curriculum, and not only in classes dealing explicitly with study of the Bible or theology. One dark day he went into the library and gathered up most of the secular LP records (no CDs back then!), including classical music, and carried them in several trips to the garbage dumpster. His explanation was that they had nothing to do with the Bible or our Bible-based curriculum.

Some evangelicals are opposed to using secular counseling or psychological theories and methods; they substitute a Bible-based counseling approach for them. One Bible college fired its professor of pastoral counseling because he used elements of behavioral conditioning to work with troubled people and taught students the theories of B. F. Skinner and other behaviorists. He didn't agree with them about everything, but he thought they had something to offer. Many evangelical children today are being home schooled. Often they spend as much time reading and studying the Bible as every other subject combined. Some Christian home schooling curricula use the Bible in every subject.

So, am I now attacking the Bible? Not at all. As an evangelical Christian I regard the Bible as my (and our!) primary source and norm for all matters of faith and spiritual practice. The voice of God speaks to us primarily through the Holy Scriptures, which are supernaturally inspired. The Bible is the supreme oracle of God, and it cannot be superseded or replaced by anything else. However, I qualify that by saying "in matters of doctrine and the practice of the Christian faith." I do not think the Bible is a source book for science, mathematics, politics, or most other subjects one studies in contemporary schools.

Some years ago a well-intentioned Christian medical doctor wrote a book entitled *None of These Diseases* (Revell, 1963), in which he described how the Bible provides guidance on living a healthy lifestyle especially in the area of diet. Many evangelical Christians took his book as evidence of the Bible's inspiration and divine authority and also tried to live by it even against their doctor's advice. An entire industry of Christian food supplements (vitamins, minerals) sprang up, and conservative Christians all over America were selling, buying, and taking them religiously. Later medical science showed that a healthy diet is sufficient for most people; they do not really need food supplements.

Folk Christianity tends to include an inordinate focus on the Bible as an oracle of God on virtually every subject of real importance. At its lowest level of sophistication folk Christianity encourages people to pray for divine guidance, drop open the Bible with eyes closed, and point to a passage. (Well, perhaps there's a lower level than that. I recently saw a news report that showed Christian contractors sealing up Bibles in the walls of new houses believing that just the physical presence of a Bible in the structure would bless the occupants and draw them to Christ!) That passage, then, becomes the answer to the problem the person was praying about.

I have known quite a few people who have testified that God answered their questions in just that way. I don't deny that God might occasionally do that. God answered Gideon's prayers even though Gideon's use of the "fleece" method is not for everyone. But the "drop and point" method of gaining guidance from Scripture is not indicative of most folk Christianity. Many folk Christians simply assume that somewhere in the Bible lies dormant and perhaps yet undiscovered the answer to every pressing moral and ethical issue. For many this extends into the realm of politics and the social ordering of society. For them, "The Bible has all the answers" means if one digs hard enough, one can find guidance and direction from God for every crucial problem faced by individuals and societies.

> **MANY** folk Christians simply assume that somewhere in the Bible lies dormant and perhaps yet undiscovered the answer to every pressing moral and ethical issue.

One evidence of this is the tendency to display the Ten Commandments in or around public schools, courthouses, and government buildings. For many conservative Christians the Decalogue (another word for the Ten Commandments) is a symbol for the Bible as a whole. When they argue for

such displays, they don't necessarily mean that government decisions and judge's rulings should be based entirely or strictly on
just that one portion of Scripture, though they probably do regard
it as especially relevant as one foundation of our "Christian society." However, it's unlikely that judges and teachers (et cetera) who
want to display the Ten Commandments in public think these ten
imperatives sum up everything one needs to know. Rather, I suspect, they think the Bible as a whole, symbolized by the Decalogue,
is or should be the foundation of community life even beyond the
borders of the church and Christian organizations. "The Bible has
all the answers." Maybe not for which brand of refrigerator to buy,
but for daily personal living and decision making and for public pol-
icy and adjudication of tough problems that come before courts.

A REFLECTIVE APPROACH TO THE BIBLE

Reflective Christianity is uncomfortable with this approach
to the Bible. It raises questions such as, "Does the Bible really
provide divine guidance for every important daily problem?" And,
"Should the Bible be regarded as a collection of divine oracles
that covers every conceivable, important, pressing issue facing
contemporary society?" Or is the Bible's scope and authority limited to identifying who God is (his nature and character) and what
God has done for us (redemption) and wants from us in terms of
spiritual living (discipleship and devotion)? Does it contain a pattern for society beyond the church? Does it even offer answers to
problems of governance? Should it be considered a source book
or book of guiding principles for science? Can we derive from it
solutions to psychological difficulties? Is there a biblical method of
counseling? Reflective Christianity raises such questions over folk
religious attitudes and treatments of the Bible. An important step
from folk Christianity to reflective Christianity is gaining a more
profound perspective on the Bible's historical and human nature
as well as its intended purpose.

Please don't misunderstand me at this point. Perhaps you
are getting nervous. You agree with me that the Bible doesn't

provide guidance about which brand of refrigerator to buy. But you do think the Bible is a book of divine oracles covering all really important issues of individual and social life. However, a close inspection of the Bible itself reveals that it does not contain all the answers to life's pressing questions. Furthermore, a closer inspection reveals that often its advice about many matters seems contradictory (especially between what God said through Old Testament prophets and what he said through Jesus!). Such close reading of the Bible shows that the human authors and their cultural contexts are very much in evidence in what the Bible says.

AN important step from folk Christianity to reflective Christianity is gaining a more profound perspective on the Bible's historical and human nature as well as its intended purpose.

The Bible often says nothing at all about matters that really do make a difference in contemporary life. The human authors were not mere "secretaries of the Holy Spirit." Their cultures and personalities are apparent in their writing. Take, for example, the apostle Paul. Read his letters and compare them with, say, John's three letters. Paul's grammar (especially in Greek, which has been "touched up" by modern translators) is not always the best. He leaves whole sentences unfinished (e.g., 1 Corinthians 12:2). Furthermore, in the heat of writing he gets things wrong occasionally and then corrects himself. (At first he thought he had baptized no one at Corinth but then he realized he had baptized a few folks there; see 1 Corinthians 1:14–16.) His temper shows through his writing. He expresses the wish that the Judaizing apostles troubling the Galatians by telling the adult men they had to be circumcised in order to be Christians would castrate themselves (Galatians 5:12). (Translations tend to soften the blow a bit!) Scholars can easily show how Paul's Greek education influenced his rhetorical style. All in all, even conservative evangelical scholars know that Paul's humanity shines through his writings. The same is true of other biblical authors. The fingerprints of humanity are all over the books of the Bible! It is not a divinely dictated book.

More to our point here, however, is the Bible's limitations as a book of divine oracles speaking to all pressing issues of personal and social life. Not only is the Bible a human book (as well as divinely inspired), it is also a religious book and not an encyclopedia of information on secular matters. One is hard pressed to show where Jesus or the writers of the New Testament ever encouraged Christians to use the Bible as a pattern for setting up Christian societies or treating people with physical or mental conditions. Praying for earthly rulers is one thing (encouraged by the New Testament), but becoming earthly rulers and using the Bible as basic law is something else. That doesn't appear in the New Testament. Pointing people into the Scriptures for spiritual wisdom and guidance and praying for their healing is one thing. Using the Bible as a textbook for medicine or psychotherapy is something else.

THE fingerprints of humanity are all over the books of the Bible! It is not a divinely dictated book.

Of course, one has to distinguish between the Old Testament and the New. Much of what we read in the Old Testament (Hebrew Bible) is meant for Israel's collective life as a society. There religious life and civil life are treated inseparably. But in light of the New Testament, do Christians have any warrant for looking back to the Old Testament for guidance in setting up contemporary civil governments? That's doubtful. Surely there would be something in the New Testament about that if it were the case.

Does the Bible help with treating schizophrenia or most other serious mental and emotional illnesses? Where? Of course, if you think such diseases are really manifestations of demon infestation (as most people of the ancient world, especially in Palestine, probably thought), then the only thing to do is exorcize the demons. Strangely, however, many folk Christians who attempt to use the Bible as a textbook for solving psychological problems don't even believe in contemporary demon possession! Even most who do believe in demon possession know that some mental illnesses are biologically based and not amenable to spiritual therapies alone.

Medicine and hospital treatment are necessary in the most extreme cases. Indicative of many folk Christians' attitudes about these matters, however, is a tendency to shun psychotherapy except in such extreme cases. But why? If medicine and intensive psychotherapy can help people who are psychotic, why not use them to help people (even Christians!) suffering from severe depression, which we now know scientifically is often the result of chemical imbalances in the brain?

The point here is simply that folk Christianity is often inconsistent. On the one hand, people say the Bible contains the answers to basic political, social, and psychological needs. But on the other hand, they realize that some such problems find no answers in Scripture and need solutions from other sources. In the realm of politics and economics, for example, who really thinks the Bible teaches democracy or capitalism? These are modern developments that find little if any support in the Bible, and yet most folk Christians value them highly. When pressed they have trouble finding them anywhere in the Bible!

In the realm of psychology many Christians think the Bible contains the answers to basic psychological problems. Yet they would be among the first to commit a truly schizophrenic person to a hospital for treatment. Why not realize that even severe marital problems can be helped by extrabiblical means? Does it have to be an either-or? Can the Bible and modern psychotherapy be combined (so long as the psychotherapy is not explicitly naturalistic)?

Folk Christianity is simply confused over these matters about the Bible and contemporary individual and social life. Reflective Christianity seeks a way out of such confusion. It recognizes that the Bible is not a textbook of anything except godliness. Its scope and authority have only to do with Christian faith and practice. It is a religious book. Where it speaks about cosmology (the make up and order of the universe), political order, psychology, and numerous other subjects, it is not to be treated as exhaustive divine oracles, and it may be mistaken by modern standards because the human authors' ancient cultural limitations and personal biases may have intruded.

The divine inspiration of Scripture was not a process of dictation that overwhelmed the authors' individual personalities, limitations, or cultural influences. It was rather an operation of God's Spirit on the authors that led them to communicate truth essential to Christian knowledge of God and salvation. Some evangelicals worry that if there is a single technical error in the whole Bible, then the Bible cannot be trusted in anything. Some fundamentalists argue that no discernable line can be found between the "spiritual" and the "nonspiritual" within Scripture. I'm not so sure about either of these concerns.

Common sense tells us that many authorities make minute errors that do not impugn their expertise or credibility in a particular subject. One or two errors in a phone book hardly make it useless. A textbook that contains a few errors (which do not?) is not considered worthless.

The plain fact of the matter is that the Bible does contain some statements that seem mistaken by modern standards of completeness and accuracy. Even the most conservative Christian scholars know this. For example, in 1 Corinthians 10:8 Paul refers to an incident in the history of ancient Israel where, he says, twenty-three thousand people died in one day. That event is recorded in Numbers 25:9, but there it says that twenty-four thousand died. There are a number of ways of finessing this if a person is determined to explain it away. But why? Why not just admit that Paul, like every other human writer of Scripture, was not giving a flawless performance in statistics? Even the most fundamentalist Bible scholars and theologians admit that the Bible *as we have it* (even the best reconstruction of the Hebrew and Greek

> **THE** divine inspiration of Scripture was not a process of dictation that overwhelmed the authors' individual personalities, limitations, or cultural influences. It was rather an operation of God's Spirit on the authors that led them to communicate truth essential to Christian knowledge of God and salvation.

manuscripts) contains errors. Only the original autographs (the original manuscripts the authors wrote on) had none—but those don't exist.

Am I arguing that belief in the inerrancy of the Bible constitutes folk Christianity? No. Many astute evangelical Bible scholars and theologians believe the Bible is inerrant, but they qualify inerrancy so that this word does not mean what many lay Christians assume it must mean. Conservative biblical scholars and theologians admit that the Bible contains what seem to be errors and that some of its statements reflect the cultures of the biblical authors.

> **THE** plain fact of the matter is that the Bible does contain some statements that seem mistaken by modern standards of completeness and accuracy.

The key difference between folk religious belief about the Bible and reflective, conservative Christian belief about the Bible's inerrancy lies in the qualifications the latter makes. Most reflective Christian believers in inerrancy urge that modern standards of technical accuracy not be imposed on the Bible; as an ancient book and one dedicated to spiritual matters, its inerrancy or infallibility has to do with its purpose. It is *perfect with respect to purpose*, but if modern standards of technical accuracy are imposed, flaws can be found in what it records even if not in what it affirms. Folk Christianity tends to assume something the vast majority of conservative evangelical Bible scholars and theologians have never believed: that when subjected to modern scientific and historical examination the Bible is found to be literally true and technically accurate about everything on which it touches.

HEARING THE MASTER'S VOICE (IN SPITE OF THE FLAWS)

I like Swiss theologian Emil Brunner's illustration of our reflective evangelical position on the Bible's authority in spite of its technical fallibility in incidental matters. Brunner appealed to the old RCA Victrola record player logo that showed a dog sitting with its head cocked toward the large end of an old Victrola record player megaphone. The caption read "His master's voice." Brunner noted that just as the dog can still hear his master's voice in spite of the scratches on an old 78 rpm record, we can still hear our master's "voice" speaking to us through the Bible in spite of its many minor flaws. The Bible's incidental errors (which are only "errors" when judged by modern standards alien to the Bible) are evidence of its humanity; the Bible isn't an idol to be worshiped any more than it is a magical book from which to draw encoded messages.

MOST reflective Christian believers in inerrancy urge that modern standards of technical accuracy not be imposed on the Bible; as an ancient book and one dedicated to spiritual matters, its inerrancy or infallibility has to do with its purpose.

The Bible is God's story, and he draws us into it in ways that transform our lives. That can happen even if it does contain flaws in matters that have nothing directly to do with the "big story" of God. I am not necessarily arguing here that the Bible does contain errors. Much depends on what one means by "error." But clearly the Bible contains human elements such as Paul's temper, bad grammar, and flawed performance in statistics. Whether one believes in biblical inerrancy or not is not the watershed between folk religion and examined faith. Rather, that lies between recognition of the Bible's humanity and folk religion's tendency to deny or minimize it.

But is it possible to discern the line between matters that pertain to salvation (i.e., spiritual matters) and those that do not? Admittedly that's not always easy. But common sense and reason can guide us in this too. Of course, prayerful reading under the leadership of the Holy Spirit is also necessary for any sound interpretation of the Bible. Is it really so difficult to identify aspects

WHETHER one believes in biblical inerrancy or not is not the watershed between folk religion and examined faith. Rather, that lies between recognition of the Bible's humanity and folk religion's tendency to deny or minimize it.

of the biblical witness that communicate something about God's character and will, redemption and discipleship? Surely not.

Or perhaps it would be better to ask if it is really so hard to identify aspects that don't. Take, for example, the lists of Old Testament kings of Judah and Israel. Who thinks an error in these would in any way affect anyone's salvation? Then there are those genealogies, including Jesus' own ancestors listed at the beginning of Matthew and Luke. What if these contain errors? Is anything important lost? Would anyone be led astray from the path of true righteousness or misidentify God? I doubt it. The main purpose of the Bible is pretty clear to everyone who studies it carefully, and church history (church fathers and Reformers) has commonly identified it as spiritual.

There may be areas where the line is not as clear as, for example, in Paul's instructions to the first-century churches about church order and leadership. There some principles seem clearly to be authoritative for all times and places while others seem to be accommodations to the culture of that time. For example, in 1 Corinthians Paul says women should cover their heads when praying "because of the angels." And men should not have long hair. Almost no one in contemporary evangelicalism thinks these are commandments for all times. So even those who say there is no clear line between the timeless spiritual truths of Scripture and other more mundane matters do seem to recognize and live by one.

Am I arguing for what some conservative evangelical theologians call "partial inspiration" of Scripture? No. All Scripture is inspired by God (2 Timothy 3:16). But "inspiration" does not mean "dictation." Rather, the Holy Spirit moved God's people (prophets and apostles) to write certain things that would convey spiritual messages. That action of the Holy Spirit did not turn the writers into mere copyists of words. Apparently they were allowed to use their own words, cultural idioms, favorite phrases, and so on, as long as the message God wanted to be conveyed shone through. Even those portions of Scripture that contain flaws (by modern standards) are inspired.

Does that make the Holy Spirit a liar? In my opinion, and I dare say in the opinions of most reflective Christians, that's ludicrous.

If I communicate a message to my teaching assistant to give to all my students and she gets one or two minor points wrong in such a way that does not affect the message, does that make me a liar? Not at all. Nor does it make her one. The Bible isn't *That Manuscript from Heaven*. It is mediated revelation from God. The fingerprints of humanity on that revelation do not nullify the truth of the gospel. In other words, I am arguing for full inspiration combined with recognition of human and cultural mediation in the Bible. To me that accords best with the actual data of Scripture. It avoids obscurantism while preserving the Bible's spiritual authority.

All that is to say that the main purpose of the Bible is what we should be concerned about grasping, living, and defending. Reflective Christianity grows out of and beyond the childish idea that the Bible has to be a magical book or a perfect book in order to be our guide to knowing God, finding salvation, and walking in God's ways. Reflective Christianity discovers and acknowledges that the Bible does not speak about many important subjects and is without flaws only in those matters that have to do with its purpose.

Reflective Christianity is more concerned with principles than with propositions (assertions of fact) and with transformation than with information. The Bible is not merely a book of information, and if some of its information is culturally conditioned that doesn't mean it cannot still be a soul-transforming book. The Bible lacks clear propositional statements that address many pressing contemporary issues. Abortion is almost absent from the Bible. Nothing there speaks directly to cremation. The thorny problems of modern economics find few if any solutions in the Bible. And what about cloning? It wasn't even envisioned by biblical authors. The point is that the Bible

THE Bible simply does not contain all the answers.

simply does not contain all the answers. For answers to many important issues we have to turn to tradition, reason, and experience, which we always use anyway when interpreting the Bible.

QUESTIONS THE BIBLE DOES NOT ANSWER

But wait a minute, some reader (probably a scholar) is saying! While the Bible may not deliver clear pronouncements about these and many more ethical and moral issues, it does contain clear principles that can and must be brought to bear on them. Indeed. I don't disagree. But that's not the same as saying it contains "all the answers." Who really thinks the Bible answers the question, "If I can clone a human person, should I?" Imagine you are a scientist working in a bioengineering laboratory in the year 2020. Cloning animals has become commonplace; it is being done by many scientists all over the world, and many medical benefits have arisen from it. Finally you have the opportunity and ability to clone a human being. You are a Christian. Should you do it?

That very question is facing people before 2020, though in the year 2006 it is doubtful that it will happen anytime soon. Too many qualms still exist and technology is not yet up to speed to assure such human cloning would not produce monstrosities. Do you turn to the Bible? Well, you won't find anything there about cloning. (Almost everyone knows this, so why do they still claim that the Bible contains all the answers? Surely people who say this mean "except those it doesn't contain!") Some biblical scholars and theologians (including Christian ethicists) argue that the Bible contains principles that will clearly guide in every such important decision whether in the realms of politics, economics, or science. But does it?

At this point I'm not sure. Yes, the Bible says human beings are created in God's image and therefore precious in God's sight. We can infer from this that every human being has dignity and worth, and from that certain inalienable rights emerge. But how to apply that to cloning? It's not clear. Some will argue that cloning is unbiblical because it usurps God's creative role in making humans. But what about in vitro fertilization and test-tube babies? And what about human procreation itself? Doesn't God work through created means to create us? It seems so. So in principle why would cloning a person usurp God's role? I don't know that it would.

Another argument is that cloning is unbiblical because people will inevitably misuse the technology. Yes, that's for sure. But they misuse all kinds of technology that the opponents of cloning do not oppose for that reason. Organ transplantation can be and is sometimes misused (e.g., through a black market of buying and selling organs). I don't think the Bible contains the answer to cloning. That doesn't mean I'm for it. Just because something can be done does not mean it should be done. The main reason I hesitate to bless the practice is that, given technology as we have it today, a significant number of seriously deformed clones would inevitably be produced before the first normal clone is made. Is the result worth the cost in human lives? I doubt it. But I realize the same argument could be made against many breakthrough surgeries and other medical treatments.

> IN short, there are urgent and pressing matters to which the Bible does not speak.

In short, there are urgent and pressing matters to which the Bible does not speak. Yes, as evangelical Christians we all believe that it contains authoritative answers for doctrine and for practical Christian living in the realm of morality. But we should grow out of thinking of the Bible as the one supernatural textbook for every important issue. The Bible identifies God for us and shapes us into godly persons as we allow the Spirit to work through it. But we cannot count on the Bible solving dilemmas of every kind. We have to turn to tradition, reason, and experience to discern the best approaches in many crucial matters.

DISCUSSION QUESTIONS

1. What was your preconceived idea of the Bible as you approached this chapter? How did the chapter's contents challenge or change your preconceived idea?

2. Can you think of any ways (other than the ones mentioned in the chapter) that Christians almost idolize the Bible or fail to recognize and acknowledge its human side?

3. What are some "fingerprints of humanity" on the Bible other than ones mentioned in the chapter? Have they bothered you before? Do they bother you now? Has your Christian upbringing predisposed you to be nervous about evidences of the Bible's humanness?

4. A great debate has raged within evangelical Christian circles about the Bible's inerrancy. Are you aware of that? What do you think about that? How important is it that the Bible be without error? Can inerrancy be combined with recognition of the Bible's humanness? How?

5. What do you think about cloning? What are some biblical principles that might provide guidance to Christians faced with that ethical issue? What if the Bible really doesn't provide such guidance? How might a reflective Christian go about making a decision whether to participate in cloning and to support it or not?

6. What other contemporary questions or issues can you think of that the Bible does not answer? What biblical principles might help Christians deal with this issue?

7. Has this chapter helped you gain a more balanced, mature perspective on the Bible, or has it just irritated you? Or do you have some other reaction to it? What is it? How has the chapter made you feel? Why?

CHAPTER 5

GOD HAS A PERFECT PLAN FOR YOUR LIFE:
SO WHAT IF YOU MISS IT?

There's probably no more prevalent folk Christian cliché among denizens of the American evangelical youth culture than this one: "God has a perfect plan for your life." To be perfectly honest, it struck fear into my teenage heart. That's partly because our church had a wonderful older lady who often testified publicly that she had missed God's wonderful plan for her life and been miserable ever since. Well, maybe not miserable—but unfulfilled and sorrowful for having missed God's plan. You see, according to her testimony God had called her as a teenager to the mission field. She was supposed to dedicate her life to foreign missions. Not right away, of course. She was supposed to go to Bible college, marry a young man with a missionary calling, and spend the rest of her life evangelizing the lost in faraway places. Instead she married a young man who walked away from his faith. She remained married to him, but always felt that God was not pleased with her. Her testimony was a warning to us younger folks not to do what she had done.

Somewhere lurking on a wall in virtually every evangelical church is a hand-stitched, framed display of Jeremiah 29:11: " 'For I know the plans I have for you,' declares the LORD, 'plans to prosper you and not to harm you, plans to give you hope and a future.' " Almost every fervently evangelical college student knows it by heart. Many have made it their "life verse." From this, under the influence of older spiritual mentors, they have drawn the conclusion that God has a blueprint for each Christian's life and finding that blueprint and working within it is a condition of being happy and fulfilled.

Back in the 1970s a nationwide evangelistic campaign used a small booklet that began with "God has a wonderful plan for your life." Countless evangelical people came to believe in this "blueprint model" of God's will. It led some of them to expect God to unfold the blueprint before their eyes as they read the Bible and prayed for guidance. When no lightening bolt came from the blue to tell them whom they should marry or which college they should attend or what their life's vocation should be, they put out fleeces: "God, if you want me to attend that college, have someone send me a check for the first semester's tuition by next Thursday." Or they would pray for God to open and shut doors: "God, if you want me to marry Jennifer, have her call me and ask me to the senior banquet."

MEANINGS OF "GOD'S WILL"

A basic difference between folk religion and reflective Christianity lies in the line between magic and prayer. Occasionally, God answers such "fleece" questions. He did it in "the Bible days"

(Gideon and others). But counting on it comes closer to magic than to having a real relationship with God.

Magic is thinking we have to manipulate God by special words or acts that are virtually guaranteed to bring him out of hiding and get him to act on our behalf. At the root of magical religious thinking is the belief that God has a secret will and a power he's holding back, waiting for us to do something special that will cause him to reveal his will

> A basic difference between folk religion and reflective Christianity lies in the line between magic and prayer.

and zap us with his power. Like everything else in folk Christianity, this magical thinking isn't entirely wrong. The problem is that it treats God too much like an object. And it treats him like a reluctant blesser or like the bad parent who says to the child, "I have a special present for you if you come up with the right word!" We think parents who tease their children that way are immature at best and abusive at worst. But many evangelicals think of God along the same lines.

Not only are some of the methods of finding God's will insulting to God (because they treat him like an object), but the whole idea of God's will as a blueprint is seriously flawed. The obsession with "finding God's perfect will" and the anxiety that inevitably accompanies it are evidence of folk Christianity; reflective Christianity raises some hard questions about these beliefs and practices and encourages maturing Christians to move beyond them toward a deeper understanding.

What are some of the questions? The first and most important ones are: Does the Bible really teach that God has a blueprint will for every individual's life? Or does that idea arise more from folk religion? Is it a manifestation of wishful thinking that actually ends up doing more harm than good? Also, one has to wonder whether there might be better, more biblical and God-honoring as well as less anxiety-creating, ideas about God's will for individuals. And might such understandings of God's will be more consistent with other beliefs most Christians hold?

Let's look first at the proof text often appealed to in support of the blueprint model: Jeremiah 29:11. A basic rule of biblical interpretation is to look at the context before deciding what a passage means. "A text pulled out of context is a pretext," the old hermeneutics and homiletics professor told his classes. Does Jeremiah 29:11 teach that God has a wonderful, detailed plan for each and every individual's life?

First, consider the context. To whom is this beautiful and reassuring promise given? Well, to Israel. (Okay, smarty-pants reader! Technically it was to Judah, the southern half of the divided kingdom of Israel and Judah. I was just testing you.) In other words, first it was to a people in a specific time and place. God planned to bless them by restoring their kingdom after exile. It was a promise of hope to a discouraged people through a reluctant prophet. Can we lift it out of that historical context and apply it to each and every individual follower of God for all time? It's original meaning doesn't warrant that.

However, Christians have a long tradition going back to Jesus and Paul of practicing a "spiritual reading" of Scripture alongside of and after a literal-historical reading. That's not exactly the same thing as what you may have heard of as "allegorical interpretation." The latter was common among some early centuries Christians; it looked for meanings in the Bible that had little or nothing to do with the literal or historical senses of passages.

Spiritual reading acknowledges that the voice of God's Spirit may use a passage (such as a promise) to encourage people far away from the original setting in both time and place. One has to be careful with this, however. The spiritual sense must be related to the literal-historical sense and has to make sense. That is, it has to be reasonable and not fanciful or exotic. All that is to say that it is not absurd for a group of Christians to use Jeremiah 29:11 as a comforting promise of God. However, because it was made to a specific group in a specific time and place, it cannot be transferred with quite the same unconditional emphasis to everyone else. Taken in light of everything else the Bible says about God and his people, it is safe to say that God does want to bless us; *his desire for us is our welfare (well-being) and not evil.* The character of God as revealed by Jesus Christ supports this. Think of the so-called Lord's Prayer (which is really better titled the Disciples' Prayer!). God is our shepherd, who supplies our needs.

However, neither Jeremiah 29:11 nor any other biblical passage teaches that God has a detailed plan for each and every individual's life. Where do people derive from it (or any other verse) the idea that God has a specific person for them to marry or a specific college for them to attend? Such meticulously detailed planning does not seem to be revealed in the Bible, and certainly not in Jeremiah 29:11!

But wait (you might be thinking or even saying out loud)! What about all those stories in the Bible where God chose people to do very specific things and almost forced them into it? Isn't Paul an example? He was named Saul and was persecuting Christians all around the ancient Middle East. Then God knocked him off his horse on the road to Damascus and dragged him kicking and screaming into being an apostle. Later, when he was on a missionary journey headed toward a place called Bithynia, God said, "No. Go to Troas instead." Wouldn't it be nice if God was so clear about his directions for all of us? But does Paul's life and ministry support the idea that God has a specific, detailed plan for everyone's life? Not necessarily.

First, Paul was a special case. Many of the people in the Bible are special cases. It is dangerous to extrapolate from what God did with David or Isaiah or Peter or Paul to what he does with every Christian. Apparently God does choose certain people for certain tasks and virtually forces them into action. Look at Jonah! God wanted him to preach to Nineveh, but he ran the opposite direction. Can we all count on being swallowed by a whale or big fish if we don't find and stick to God's divine blueprint? Is that ordinary Christian existence? Or is it the case only with a few people whom God especially selects for special ministries?

Think about how miserable most of those people were! Do you really want to experience all that? Well, you might if God calls you into special service. Even then, however, it may not be the case that God has only one thing for you to do and if you don't do it, the rest of your life will be a spiritual wipeout. Let me suggest that for most Christians God never does knock them off a horse, show them bright lights, and speak to them audibly. Most Christians will never be swallowed by a whale or have anything similarly dramatic happen to them. In fact, maybe most Christians get to partner with God in deciding how they will serve him. Jeremiah 29:11 only says that God wants to bless and not curse his people. It doesn't say that his "plan" includes a detailed blueprint for every decision they will make.

PROBLEMS WITH THE BLUEPRINT MODEL

The idea that God has a detailed, blueprint-like plan for every individual Christian's life is not biblically supported, nor is it reasonable. Think about it for a moment. If God has such a plan, is it based on what he knows you will do or will you do it because God moves you along it as you go? In either case it doesn't seem possible for you to "miss the will of God." Or maybe God has a blueprint for your life but just knows you will mess it up by making wrong decisions (or fulfill it perfectly!).

In any case, there seems to be a mismatch between two parts of this picture. First, God has a blueprint for your life. Second, you have decisions to make and either will or will not build a life according to God's blueprint. Why would God have a blueprint for your life *that you are supposed to discover and live by* if he already knows (as most Christians believe) your entire future?

> THE idea that God has a detailed, blueprint-like plan for every individual Christian's life is not biblically supported, nor is it reasonable.

Wouldn't the "real blueprint" be what God knows you will do and not what you should but don't do? Combined with the foreknowledge of God, the old blueprint model of God's will becomes shaky at best. Moreover, it creates a lot of anxiety and confusion. Doesn't God already know whom you will marry? What does "finding his will" mean in that scenario? Why struggle so much if it's already all laid out in God's future vision?

But what if God has a blueprint for your life but somehow hides from himself whether or not you will live according to it? (A group of evangelicals called open theists believe God limits his knowledge so that he does not always already know every future free decision a person will make.) Then the anxiety really mounts! What happens if you don't "find" and "live according to" God's blueprint? What if you marry the wrong person? What if you go to the wrong college? What if you enter the wrong life vocation? What if you discover ten years down the road that God wanted you to be a foreign missionary and you became an accountant?

Well, the mind boggles. The old blueprint model of God's will leads into all kinds of conundrums and emotional dead-ends. It creates spiritual bondage where there should be liberty. And it just doesn't make sense. Surely if you miss the will of God in one area of your life, God mercifully and graciously opens up new possibilities. The blueprint model has to be expanded to be more flexible. As it is, it's just too rigid—and it's legalistic. So, let's see if there might be a better model. But we'll get there eventually. Before laying out a better model for understanding God's will, we need to consider the God-person relationship a bit more.

First, God is a loving person and not a computer who spits out unalterable equations. When we go to God in prayer asking for guidance and direction, we should not picture ourselves sitting down at a computer entering *mapquest.com* and finding a map of our destination with detailed directions for getting from here to there. All that's too impersonal and objectifying (in that it treats God and our relationship with him as an object). God is a person and not a machine or a computer program. We are persons. The God-person relationship is an intensely personal one (which does not necessarily mean "individualistic"). There's a special quality to personal relationships that is lacking in a relationship between a person and a computer—care, concern, flexibility, interaction, communion.

These all characterize what Swiss theologian Emil Brunner called (borrowing from Jewish philosopher Martin Buber) the "I-Thou" relationship as opposed to the "I-It" relationship. An I-Thou relationship should involve no manipulation. When manipulation enters the picture, the I-Thou relationship moves toward an I-It relationship. Thinking of God along the lines of a blueprint maker does not do justice to his caring, personal side or his respect for us as persons.

If I want to know what my spouse wants me to do on Saturday, I don't plead with her for a detailed list of projects and directions. I enter into conversation with her about my plans and hers, what needs to be done that I don't know about, and how might I use the time, talents, and tools I have to be helpful. I have a friend who once tried leaving lists of things for his wife to do around the house. Needless to say, it didn't go over very well. Persons communicate with each other and enter into interactive mutual planning with each other. One might be the superior partner in the process as in the case of a parent and child. But if it is a loving and caring relationship, one does not dominate and manipulate the other one.

There's something manipulative and uncaring about the blueprint model of God's will. If we are developing a personal relationship with God, surely God's will for the details of our lives is more flexible than that. Surely it leaves room for our proposals and free partnership with God in finding paths of fulfillment and service. Why would our heavenly Father determine to bless only one possible course of life? Why would he pick out and leave us to find one person to marry such that if we mistakenly marry someone else our life will be miserable? Now, of course, if you still think that God "zaps" people with absolute certainty about whom to marry, then this argument isn't going to help you much. But if that's your belief, I pity you. Someday you're going to pray and pray and pray and the heavens will remain as brass—closed to that kind of hoped-for and expected supernatural revelation. Everyone experiences that eventually.

My argument here assumes that you — my reader — have already experienced (or know of someone experiencing) the frustration and anxiety of trying to discover God's "perfect will" in some life decision and failing to receive the sought-for bolt out of the blue that leaves no doubt about which way to go. That's the experience of most Christians laboring under the burden of the blueprint model. Now, of course, if God does leave no doubt about the decision — great! I would be the last person to say that never happens. In fact, I believe it has happened to me once or twice. But the ordinary experience is otherwise. Most of the time I seek God's will according to a different model than the blueprint.

Reflective Christianity sees the difficulties with the blueprint model of God's will while acknowledging that God is God and therefore may at times act in unusual ways to move people toward a specific goal he has in mind for them. To think of God's will as always and for every person a predetermined blueprint, however, raises more questions than it answers and creates tremendous anxiety and sometimes even frustration to the point of despair. What happens if I step off and away from the blueprint? Am I forever outside of God's will? Do I have any say at all in how my life as a Christian will go? Or is God the all-determining puppet master who pulls my strings? (We already considered and rejected that model of God's interaction with us in chapter 2!) What if I accidentally marry the wrong person? Is there only one person God wants me to marry? What if I accept a job that's not the one God has for me? Will I then be a failure? Does God really have one career laid out for me and, if so, why is finding it so hard?

> TO think of God's will as always and for every person a predetermined blueprint, however, raises more questions than it answers and creates tremendous anxiety and sometimes even frustration to the point of despair.

These questions can result in one of two responses — or perhaps one and then the other in that order. First, they can drive one to despair so that the person gives up entirely on finding God's will or lives in endless anxiety and despondency, fearing he or she has missed it. Second, such people can alter their understanding of God's will and finding that will to a slightly more ambiguous but less unsettling model. Many reflective Christians have found tremendous liberation in scrapping the blueprint model and discovering the "canvas and paints" model of God's will.

THE CANVAS-AND-PAINTS MODEL

Instead of thinking of God's will as a blueprint and the person seeking God's will as a partially blind person struggling to read the blueprint and live by it, why not think of it as a canvas and set of paints? The person seeking God's will becomes, then, a painter—perhaps an amateur painter, but a painter nevertheless. The canvas stands for a person's life. God gives us a life—a particular life starting with parents, genetic inheritance, language and culture, geographical location, relatives and friends, schools, and experiences. The future beginning with each day is the canvas. It includes the contours of your particular life.

Then God gives the paints and the paintbrushes, which symbolize his gifts—strengths, talents, God's Word, mentors, human models (teachers, pastors, etc.), and opportunities. Then God says, "Paint me a beautiful picture." Oh, and he gives us the Holy Spirit as an art instructor and Jesus Christ as model. (Of course, Jesus is much more than just a human model; he is our Savior. But for purposes of this analogy he is our model.) But we're not just supposed to paint Jesus. We're supposed to paint a life that is our own modeled on the character of Jesus. God will help us. Each day we fill in a little bit of the painting. We make mistakes and have to make corrections to the painting.

In other words, God's will is not necessarily a foreordained blueprint that God leaves you to discover and follow in constructing the edifice of your life. It may be like that at times. But those exceptional occasions can be fitted into the canvas-and-paints model. Suppose you are painting along, developing a beautiful picture, and suddenly it is as if you see a section of the canvas that looks like one of those old "paint by numbers" sets found in hobby stores. (My grandmother used to paint landscapes using paint-by-numbers sets she bought; they were framed and hung all over her house.) Most of the canvas doesn't have these on it. But just as you are approaching an upper corner and about to paint a cloud, you discern some little funny shaped boxes of different sizes with numbers in them. You notice some of your paints have numbers on them. Aha! Someone wants you to paint something else there and not a cloud!

You see, I think that if God wants you to do something specific, he will find a way to let you know as long as you are painting with his colors. That is, as long as your entire painting project is saturated with prayer and seeking to honor God using what you know, he will show you when and if he wants you to paint a certain portion in a certain way. God is not tricky. He's not into leaving us to our own devices when he wants something specific from us.

Most often older Christians testify that they can discern God's will as they look back on their lives. It seems to them like a mixture of their own efforts at sound decision making and God's Spirit moving them along in certain directions. But they didn't wait for God's lightening bolt of direction and guidance to hit them before they made a decision. They trusted God to use their minds as they weighed options and stepped out in faith in certain directions.

What God is mainly concerned about most often is our character. When we talk about God's will for life, we mean living a life that is God-honoring and Christlike. Occasionally we also mean a specific plan for a specific time and place. But being who he is, faithful and good, God will not hide that and make you search for it like a blind person in a maze. It may be that God has a specific person for you to marry or a specific college you should attend. But if so, he'll leave little doubt about that if you are faithfully painting your canvas using the gifts he's giving you and allowing the Holy Spirit to help.

For most Christians, however, God may not have specific spouses already set aside for them. He probably really doesn't care which college of several they choose. His concern is that whichever person they marry and whichever college they attend, they fit that into the beautiful life they are painting for him. In other words, with his help they make the best of it.

Of course, the canvas-and-paints model does not mean that God's will is compatible with anything and everything. If God's will isn't ordinarily a blueprint, neither is it a mess. It is bounded by and founded on revealed principles of character and conduct. Part of finding God's will is living within a spiritual community that helps us with our painting project.

When I was in elementary school, my art teacher selected me to attend a special art class at the city's art center on Saturdays. There I learned a lot of about painting and drawing and making sculptures — as much from other students as from the teachers. I worked in small groups where many of my fellow artists were older and more talented and experienced. They critiqued my work and showed me how to improve it. I watched them at work and learned techniques I never would have discovered on my own. So it is with painting a life according to God's will. We shouldn't think of that as an isolated, individual task. Not only do we have the Holy Spirit and Jesus Christ to help us, but we also need and should have other painters around us. That is the body of Christ, the church. The first step in finding God's will is being seriously plugged in to a vital community of God's people who are all involved in finding and doing God's will. We need to seek out and accept the help of experienced and trained spiritual professionals when the time comes to make certain decisions.

> **IF** God's will isn't ordinarily a blueprint, neither is it a mess. It is bounded by and founded on revealed principles of character and conduct.

FINDING GOD'S WILL REFLECTIVELY

When I was in seminary I struggled with my call to ministry. Should I be a pastor? Most of my fellow students were studying to be that. Or should I aim to be a professor at a Christian college or seminary? One tool God used to help me make this important life decision was a professor of psychology and an aptitude test he administered. After students took the test, he went over the results with us. Mine showed something very clearly. There was no doubt about it. My gifts, interests, and aptitudes were in the quadrant designated "research, scholarship, and teaching." My score in the section identified as pastoral was very low. This wasn't God supernaturally hitting me with a lightening bolt of direction from out of the blue. It was God using a natural, almost secular, means to speak to me about how I could best use my paints to create a beautiful picture for him. Thank God I availed myself of this means and didn't shun it just because it was seemingly secular and not "spiritual" (as I thought of spiritual then).

As I described in chapter 4, I have come to see that many important and helpful answers to life's problems can be provided by extrabiblical sources. My psychology professor was helpful in interpreting the test and making some decisions based on it. I applied to some PhD programs in theology and religious studies and asked God to open and close doors. Two "doors" remained open. I had to choose which university to attend. No great message from God was pointing clearly toward one door, so I investigated both thoroughly. I visited both departments at the respective universities and spoke with chairmen and professors and students at length. I asked people who knew a lot about universities and these particular ones especially, and they helped me sort out which one was best.

I now believe God didn't really care all that much which one I chose. He wanted my participation in this decision and he intended to work with me to make the very best of whichever one I chose. I chose one and went there and never looked back regretfully or wondered, "Is this really God's will?" The other one might have worked out just as well. The one I did attend worked out great.

> **GOD** calls us to be created cocreators of culture and church and our individual lives.

Reflective Christianity looks at the issue of God's will in light of all we know about ourselves and God. God wants us to participate with him in making our lives. That's because he is interested in an I-Thou relationship with us and not in treating us like instruments or in our treating him like an object. He calls us to be created cocreators of culture and church and our individual lives. Life is ambiguous and requires involvement and risk. You can't just sit around waiting for God's clear and unequivocal direction before making some choices. God can be trusted. If he doesn't knock you off your horse (as with Paul on the road to Damascus), then he's waiting for you to pick up your box of paints and brushes and start filling in the canvas.

DISCUSSION QUESTIONS

1. Have you been operating out of the "blueprint model" of God's plan for your life? How has that made you feel? What questions have you had about it? What do you think about it after reading this chapter?

2. A Christian university professor of computer programming once said that he pictures God as a great cosmic computer. What do you think about that idea of God?

3. Has God ever guided you in a special, undeniable way? When and how? Do you think that's the way God always communicates his will?

4. What do you think about open theism? Is it heresy? Why or why not? What are some pros and cons of this new evangelical view of God's foreknowledge?

5. What do you think of the "canvas and paints" model of God's will? What feelings does it provoke in you when you consider it as an alternative to the blueprint model? What are its merits and demerits?

6. Do you think there is always one option that God wants you to choose when presented with a choice between two or more options? Or do you agree that sometimes God doesn't really care that much which you choose (so long as it is consistent with faith in and commitment to the lordship of Jesus Christ) and leaves it entirely up to you? How does this freedom of choice make you feel?

We've all heard it said that "God helps those who help themselves." There is no more quintessential folk religious cliché. In some ways it stands opposed to the folk religious slogan dealt with in the last chapter ("God has a perfect plan for your life"), although one could combine them by saying that you can find God's will best by proving to him that you are seeking it with all your might. In any case, this platitude is uttered every day by millions of people. Not all of them are Christians; in fact, the saying is not really Christian at all. It has seeped into Christianity from folk culture. A case can be made that it is actually an alternative to Christianity. And yet countless Christians repeat it with sincerity and conviction. Some even believe it is in the Bible! They are often astounded to learn it isn't there at all. There's no verse in the Bible that can even be fairly paraphrased that way. But, for better or worse, it has become part of the common stock of American folk religion and folk Christianity. In fact, I would argue it sums up the essence of American folk religion nicely in a nutshell.

So what do people mean when they utter "God helps those who help themselves"? The statement is actually somewhat vague. People think they know what it means, but possibly that's because they haven't really examined its various possible senses. Reflective Christianity takes such a commonly repeated cliché and critically examines it. It raises questions about it, beginning with, "What does it really mean?" Let's look at it carefully.

If I say that God helps those who help themselves, I might mean only that most of the time and in most circumstances God expects people to do what they can for themselves and then he steps in to do for them what they can't do. In fact, I suspect that's what most people mean by it. But what kind of God does this sentiment depict? A somewhat reluctant God? A distant God? A God who tests us for self-reliance? A God much like some parents (the kind considered less than nurturing in many cases)? How does the sentiment expressed in the cliché depict human beings? As capable of self-reliance if not given too much help? As able to pull themselves up by their own bootstraps? As needing challenge to work hard that is undermined by too much help?

THE AMERICAN WORK ETHIC AND FOLK RELIGION

Isn't this the American way? About a century ago a popular series of dime books featured the adventures of a fictional boy named Horatio Alger. Horatio was a poor boy who made it big; he became a success through hard work with very little luck or help from others. The Horatio Alger myth has sunk deeply into the American psyche. Most Americans tend to believe that success comes from hard work and that a helping hand too early or given too eagerly undermines self-reliance and "pluck" (which is an old term for individual stick-to-itiveness). We like to believe that people who succeed in life did it by themselves through individual effort and that giving people handouts of any kind robs them of their own initiative and makes them lazy.

There's some truth to it, isn't there? For many this formula has worked well. For others, however, it has contributed to their being stuck in a cycle of poverty and hopelessness. In most cases you have to start with something in order to gain more. I fear that in many cases "God helps those who help themselves" is little more than an excuse for not helping people in need. It's a way of saying, "I'll help them (or society should help them) only if I see them pulling themselves up by their own bootstraps and beginning to make some progress toward success." That attitude leaves many of America's poorest stuck where they are.

Another question we might ask about this cliché is its context. It's always helpful to know the setting of a statement when trying to interpret it. If someone says, "Well, you know, God helps those who help themselves," when talking about people who have the means and wherewithal to make use of education or medicine or government assistance, most people would agree. Common sense tells us that when help is available, people are expected to avail themselves of it. If someone says, "You know, God helps those who help themselves," when justifying looting (such as happened during the recent hurricane in New Orleans), most people would disagree. This is the wrong kind of "helping onself." If "God helps those who help themselves" is nothing more than a statement that people need to make use of legitimate help when it is offered, then it seems noncontroversial. In that sense I affirm it and so do most people. But if it is justification for thievery of any kind or for refusing to help people truly in need, I strongly disagree with it.

But what about this slogan's application to religious life and to spirituality? That's what concerns me most here—and it should concern you. By including God in it the cliché implies a spiritual application whether everyone who utters it means that or not. When it enters into religious life, it is often interpreted as meaning that God awaits our initiative and then responds with grace. Grace here is understood as unmerited favor and help. I suspect that when many people say that God helps those who help themselves, they mean the same as the longer cliché, "If you take one step toward God he will take a step toward you."

In other words, so this folk religious sentiment goes, if someone wants God's forgiveness and strength to overcome temptation or receive a blessing from God, that person should do something first to prove sincerity and at least a modicum of self-reliance. This is the Horatio Alger myth applied to spiritual life. It's the American religion. After all, don't most evangelicals (and perhaps others) sing, "If you'll take one step toward the Savior, my friend, you'll find his arms open wide" (the second verse to Ralph Carmichael's famous contemporary Christian song "The Savior Is Waiting")? This isn't necessarily wrong. The Bible does urge people to do something for their salvation. In the famous "paradox of grace" passage of Philippians 2:12–13 Paul says "work out your salvation with fear and trembling." Clearly God expects us to do a task to have and keep our salvation.

THE PARADOX OF GRACE

The problem is that many people ignore the next part of the "paradox of grace" passage. Paul immediately follows "work out your own salvation with fear and trembling" with "for God is at work in you to will and to act to fulfill his good purpose." Both sides of the paradox must be emphasized equally. Swiss Christian theologian Emil Brunner has said that salvation is both "gift" and "task." In German this is a play on words: *Gabe* (gift) and *Aufgabe* (task). Salvation is both *Gabe* and *Aufgabe*.

How can it be both? And doesn't it mean that we have to do our work *first* and then God does his work in response to ours? That's the impression many people get from popular preaching and especially from revivalism. There's the call to response—repent and trust in Christ and you will be saved! It leaves the impression that God's work is after ours. That implies that our task is autonomous, that it is totally our own to do without any help from God. Many people take this misinterpretation into their Christian lives and live as if whatever help they get from God to live a holy life or a life of discipleship comes in measure to their own hard work.

But the Swiss theologian who emphasized salvation as both *Gabe* and *Aufgabe* was not prioritizing them the way most folk Christians do. It's our American rugged individualism with its emphasis on self-reliance and revivalist preaching that makes us think the "task" side of salvation and being a Christian comes first and is independent of the "gift" side. According to classical Christian teaching, however, that's putting the cart before the horse. When Paul told the Philippian Christians to work out their own salvation, he meant do it *because God is at work in you*, not *because God will do his work if you do yours first*.

> IT'S our American rugged individualism with its emphasis on self-reliance and revivalist preaching that makes us think the "task" side of salvation and being a Christian comes first and is independent of the "gift" side.

That seems counterintuitive to us, doesn't it? We think God's work and our work are set over against each other; that the more active I am the less active God is in me, and that the more active God is the less active I am. Or, to put it another way and more specifically, we think that God's work must necessarily follow my work; he begins where I leave off. Even popular television shows influence us to think like this. In one popular series, an angel (appearing as a human) told a man who believed God could never forgive him, that if he would only climb up toward God as far as he could go, God would reach down and take him the rest of the way (to salvation). But this is sheer folk religion. It has nothing at all to do with authentic Christianity.

Here's why our cliché and its interpretation and application in folk Christianity is wrong. If there's anything clear in the Bible it is that we human beings are, as a friend of mine likes to say, "pond scum." Oh yes, we were created in God's image. But now, because of our fallen condition, we are pond scum. The Bible puts it in terms of our corruption. Psalm 14:1 says, "They [humans] are corrupt, their deeds are vile; there is no one who does good." Romans 3:10–11 (referring back to Psalm 14) says, "There is no one righteous, not even one; there is no one who understands [God or God's ways]; there is no one who seeks God."

The picture of humanity painted by Scripture is pretty dismal. Christian theologians have called it "total depravity." It's a picture of spiritual helplessness, inability even to will the good, inability to avoid sin and evil. The Old Testament prophet Jeremiah spoke truly when he reported, "The heart is deceitful above all things and beyond cure. Who can understand it?" (Jeremiah 17:9). This biblical doctrine of our human condition under sin is unpopular because it conflicts with our belief that self-esteem is every person's birthright and most important need. That's a modern, secular belief. Of course some people need their self-esteem boosted, and telling them they are created in God's image and loved by God is true and helpful. But everyone needs to know that they are fallen and helpless and can't get up (spiritually) without God's help.

> **EVERYONE** needs to know that they are fallen and helpless and can't get up (spiritually) without God's help.

This doctrine of original sin (fallenness) and total depravity is widely misunderstood (where people even know about it!). In order to correct folk Christianity we need to take a detour through some of church history and the history of Christian teaching about humanity. Hang in there; don't give up just because the going may get a little rough. You'll learn some interesting things if you persevere.

The church father Augustine (354–430) thought deeply about the human condition based on Scripture and his own observations of human existence and behavior. In his *Confessions* he related how at a very early age he stole pears from a neighbor's orchard just for the fun of doing what was forbidden. He didn't think he was any worse than anyone else and found an explanation in the Bible. In Romans 5 Paul says we are all sinners and die because we are sinners. Augustine recognized himself in that teaching of universal sin, guilt, and death and argued that nobody can even approach God without God's prompting and enabling. That work of God within a sinner—prompting and enabling him or her to exercise a good will toward God—is called "prevenient grace."

"Prevenient" simply means "going before." It is the grace of God, a work of the Holy Spirit, that convicts sinners of their sinfulness, calls them to repent, illumines their minds and hearts about their need and God's offer of free grace, and enables them to reach out to God with sorrow and trust. It is part of the *Gabe* (gift) of God in salvation. The *Aufgabe* (humans' task) is simply to accept God's grace and let it do all the work. That accepting and "letting" involves contrition (sorrow) for sin and trust in Jesus Christ for every spiritual benefit. It involves letting go of our own efforts and letting God do the work (or apply the work he has already done on the cross!).

Augustine's view of human nature was accepted by most Christians down through the centuries because it fit perfectly with both the Bible and manifest experience. When left to their own devices people find it easier to be bad than to be good. The great English Christian commentator G. K. Chesterton said that original sin is the only empirically provable doctrine of the Christian faith. Look around. Look within. Paul asked the Corinthi-

> **ORIGINAL** sin is the only empirically provable doctrine of the Christian faith.

ans, "What do you have that you did not receive? And if you did receive it, why do you boast as though you did not?" (1 Corinthians 4:7). What real good thing does anyone have that he or she has not received?

Augustine rightly insisted against some other Christians that every spiritual good, including the first exercise of a good will toward God, is a gift of God. Because we are all sinful and corrupt, we are incapable of doing anything that would contribute in the slightest to our own salvation or even to our good accomplishments as Christians. God does it all in and through us—but not without our cooperation. Augustine said that God saves us by himself but not without us. Building on Paul's statement to the Corinthians and his own Christian experience, Augustine prayed this prayer and taught the people of his church in North Africa to pray it: "O God, command whatever you will but give whatever you command." In other words, "I'm helpless to do anything pleasing to you, so give me your grace so that I can please you." By "grace" Augustine clearly meant more than just forgiveness; he meant prevenient, assisting grace that goes before and makes possible spiritual efforts and accomplishments.

THE DEFAULT HERESY OF AMERICAN FOLK CHRISTIANITY

A monk from Britain named Pelagius came to Rome and heard Christians there repeating Augustine's prayer. He objected and wrote a book criticizing Augustine's beliefs. To make a long story short, the churches of the Roman Empire condemned Pelagius's denial of original sin and total depravity because he argued that humans are capable of pleasing God even without any special, supernatural divine assistance. Augustine responded to Pelagius that if what he taught was right, the cross would not be necessary. That Christ died for everyone proves that we are not capable of "helping ourselves."

Later, however, a milder form of Pelagius's heresy arose within the church. It came to be known as "semi-Pelagianism" because it agreed with Augustine that we need God's special grace to be saved, but it agreed with Pelagius that we can and must do something to obtain salvation. The "something" we must do (our task) is to exercise a good will toward God—and we can do that independently of God's grace. In other words, semi-Pelagianism taught (and teaches) that "if you take a step toward God, he'll take a step toward you." The initiative in salvation is ours, not God's. Salvation is God's gracious response to our autonomous approach to God with repentance and faith.

Semi-Pelagianism was condemned as heresy by the bishops of the Western, Latin Christian churches at a council in the French city of Orange in 529. That's because the Bible clearly says that we are incapable of and unwilling to exercise a good will toward God. "No one seeks for God." Also, anything good that we have is given by God. "What have you that you did not receive?" During the Protestant Reformation all the Reformers agreed that both Pelagianism and semi-Pelagianism are heresies because they undermine the grace of God and elevate human spiritual ability. They place the "task" side of salvation over against the "gift" side and prior to it. That seems to make God beholden to human beings. It is as if our action can force the grace of God, and it implies that we do have some innate spiritual goodness to which God's gift of grace is a reward. If that were true, of course, salvation would not be a sheer gift and we could boast.

> **THE** Bible clearly says that we are incapable of and unwilling to exercise a good will toward God.

The church's teaching has been, then, that the gift side of salvation precedes the task side and undergirds it. We must do something, but even what we must do (task) is enabled by God's gift of grace. Apart from God's prevenient, assisting grace we would never reach out to God or take a step toward him. We would perhaps have a restless searching for a god, but as the Reformer John Calvin said, apart from grace the human mind is but a factory of idols.

Astute readers will wonder if I'm teaching Calvinism here. That would seem to conflict with what I wrote about God and history in chapter 2. Actually, I'm not promoting Calvinism. The Roman Catholic church, which is far from Calvinistic in its theology, has at least since 529 insisted on the prevenience of grace to any and every spiritual good that human persons do. So have all Protestants unless they have fallen into folk Christianity, which is usually semi-Pelagian. I would go

> **APART** from God's prevenient, assisting grace we would never reach out to God or take a step toward him.

so far as to argue that semi-Pelagianism is the default theology of most evangelical Protestants (and Catholics). But both Calvinist and Arminian evangelical theologians oppose it with all their might. (Arminianism is the Protestant alternative to Calvinism; it takes its name from Dutch theologian Jacob Arminius, who died in 1609. He taught free will enabled by prevenient grace whereas Calvinism teaches that grace is irresistible.)

PREVENIENT GRACE

The account of human work (task) and God's gift (grace) given here is consistent with classical Arminian theology. The only place where it differs from Calvinism is that the latter believes prevenient grace is always irresistible and given only to those whom God has selected to save out of the "mass of perdition" of humanity. "God helps those who help themselves" is wrong because God loved us and began working for our salvation long before we did anything. He sent Christ to die for our sins. He released the Holy Spirit into the world to draw people to Christ. Through the proclamation of God's Word the Spirit draws people to repent and believe in Christ and enables them to be converted. If they exercise the beginning of a good will toward God, it is because of grace working in their lives whether they are aware of that or not. If a person sets out on a "search for God" and discovers God on the way (à la C. S. Lewis), it is because God first encountered them and drew them toward himself. People may be totally unaware of the secret working of God's Spirit as he aids them in their search or as he enables their response to God's Word. But we know from Scripture that is the case.

Calvinists will inevitably raise an objection here. They will agree with me that "God helps those who help themselves" is false when uttered in the context of spirituality. They will heartily endorse much of what I have said about prevenient grace. But they will want to go further and say that God's assisting grace is irresistible and given irresistibly only to the elect—those predestined by God to salvation. I'm not saying that, but this is no place (given limitations of space) to get into all the ins and outs of the debate. I believe prevenient grace is resistible even by people God intends to save and for whom Christ died.

A smart Calvinist will ask me (and you if you talk to one and agree with me) how salvation can be a free gift if a person must freely accept it. In other words, if salvation is all of grace and not at all of our own efforts (as Paul says in Ephesians 2:8), how can it be based at all on our cooperation? Wouldn't a person who could but didn't resist the grace of God unto salvation boast? In other words, a smart Calvinist will probably be trained to think that even I am falling prey to folk Christianity and implicitly agreeing that God helps those who help themselves (by not resisting God's grace).

So what do I have to say for myself? It seems to me (and I hope to you as well) that merely accepting a gift freely is not a good work. Suppose you're a broke beggar about to starve. A generous person comes along and gives you a certified check made out to you for one million dollars. (Way back in the 1950s there was a television show called *The Millionaire*, in which a very rich man gave away one million dollars in every episode. Unfortunately it was fiction!) All you have to do to have one million dollars is cash the check. You walk to the bank, endorse the check, and deposit it in your own account. Have you earned the gift? Is it no longer a gift? Yet you did something (task). You accepted the gift. Let's push the analogy a bit further. Suppose you're handicapped and can't walk to the bank. The giver of the gift brings you a wheelchair and pushes you to the bank and up to the teller's window and confirms that he gave you the check and wants you to have the money. All you have to do is write your name on the check and deposit it. Then it's yours.

Who in their right mind would say you earned the money even in part? What person in such a position would boast of having accepted the money? People would think he was insane! So it is with salvation as both gift and task. The gift precedes the task. It's God's conviction, calling, illumination, and enablement. It is the loosening of the shackles that bind your will to sin. It is God's liberation of your will to freely decide either to accept or reject his offer of free salvation. Your only task is to meet the condition of accepting the rest of God's work—Christ's death for you as your only hope of salvation. This includes, of course, admitting you're a sinner and can't do it for yourself (which is why many people resist it). It includes trusting in Christ alone. None of that is "work" in the sense of merit; none of it involves compelling grace so that you can then boast that you earned part of your salvation. It is not resisting that is hard for many people to do. We'd rather do some of it ourselves, but God won't accept us on those terms. We want to be able to boast, but in that case salvation will not be ours.

Let me try out a homely illustration on you. Imagine that we humans are fallen into a deep pit (sin) with steep and slippery sides. We're helpless to free ourselves but must get free or we'll die. There are three Christian views of how we get out of the pit. The semi-Pelagian says God throws a rope down into the pit and says, "Grab the rope and start pulling yourself up and then I'll pull from up here and together we'll get you out." The Calvinist says God throws a rope down into the pit and comes down on the rope, ties it around some people (the elect), and carries them out without their help or cooperation. Once they get out of the pit he gives them mouth-to-mouth resuscitation and revives them. They do absolutely nothing.

The Arminian says God pours water into the pit and says, "Float!" All people have to do to get out of the pit is allow the water to do its work—lift them out of the pit. That means not resisting it by holding onto things at the bottom of the pit or struggling against the water. If people get out of the pit, the water did all the work. All they had to do is let it lift them up and out by relaxing and floating on it. That "relaxing" is a picture of admitting our need for God to do everything for us because we are helpless sinners. Yes, we have to make a decision. Yes, we have to do the "work" (which is not really work at all) of allowing God to save us. But the initiative and power are all from God.

Well, no doubt the analogy has its limits. All analogies do. But

I ask you which is a more biblical picture of salvation as both gift and task? "For it is by grace you have been saved, through faith—-and this is not from yourselves, it is the gift of God—not by works, so that no one can boast" (Ephesians 2:8–9). Grace is God's provision and includes everything saving. Faith is our contribution, which is simply receiving and not resisting God's provision. Grace goes before (prevenient) and enables even our faith.

In a sense, then, even faith is a gift although we have to exercise it. Suppose someone gives me the gift of a watch. Now I can tell what time it is—but only by looking at the watch! Another homely illustration, but it helps illustrate (however imperfectly) how faith can be both gift and task. Without prevenient grace I can't have faith; I would never exercise faith. But with prevenient grace I am able and required to do something—trust in Christ alone. That's not an autonomous work; it is simply using the gift God has provided.

"God helps those who help themselves." "If you take a step toward God, he'll take a step toward you." Wrong. Both are wrong. And so are the numerous other pleasant but false clichés so many Christians and others use to express the gift and task duality of salvation. Yes, salvation is a cooperative project, but God is the infinitely superior power enabling anything that we contribute. And our contribution is meager and measly and negligible compared with grace. It's probably best not to call it a "contribution" as that inevitably implies a good work and ability to boast. All that we do is allow God to do his work in us.

OUR HUMAN ROLE IN RECEIVING GRACE

How does all this apply to the Christian life after initial salvation (conversion)? The same principle applies there; it is all of grace, but we have to let grace work holiness in us. You see, there are no "grace boosters." Grace cannot be boosted. We can't get "more grace" by doing things whether it be church participation, tithing, witnessing, or partaking of the sacraments. God's grace in a Christian's life is as full as it can possibly be.

Then why do so many Christians live defeated lives where grace is nowhere in evidence? Let me use another homely illustration. When I water the plants in my yard, I haul the garden hose out to the plants and press the "trigger" on the end nozzle to start the water spray. But usually at that point nothing happens. I go back and make sure the faucet is turned on all the way. It is. I go back and press the trigger again. Still nothing. Then I realize there's a kink in the hose. I go back looking for it and straighten out the hose, in which case it fills with water to the nozzle; when I press the trigger the water shoots out onto the plants. You see, the water (grace) was on all the way. It wasn't getting to the nozzle because of a stoppage in the hose (sin in my life). When I pray and admit my sin and ask the Holy Spirit to remove it from my life (getting the kink out of the hose), God's grace is able to flow.

The only problem with this illustration is that it doesn't do justice to the fact that even my prayer is prompted and enabled by grace. Still, the point is that if my Christian life is one of defeat and not victory over the world, the flesh, and the devil, it is not because of any insufficiency in God's grace. It is because I am not doing my part of asking and allowing God to remove the things in my life that block the flow of grace. Gift and task. Mostly gift; a little bit task. All gift because even the task is enabled by God.

DISCUSSION QUESTIONS

1. Have you ever heard or thought that God helps those who help themselves? What did you (or the people you know who said this) mean by the statement? After reading this chapter what do you think about it?

2. Have you encountered any other manifestations of semi-Pelagianism (or outright Pelagianism) than what is discussed in this chapter? What were they? Why are they semi-Pelagian (or just plain Pelagian)?

3. Do you agree that in our natural, fallen state (apart from God's grace) we human beings are "pond scum"? Why or why not?

4. Where, when, and how has God's prevenient grace worked in your life? Or do you think God's grace has come in response to your willing initiative?

5. What do you think about this chapter's "pit" analogy to the human predicament and God's response with prevenient grace? Does it help you understand how God's work and ours can cooperate without making salvation meritorious (i.e., something the saved person could boast of)?

6. What do you think about the model of grace and human response outlined in this chapter? Does this chapter do justice to God's grace or (as some might object) does it diminish grace and elevate the human contribution to salvation too much? Or is it the other way around — does it perhaps diminish the human contribution and elevate the divine? Or does it achieve a balance?

CHAPTER 7

JESUS IS COMING SOON:

SO WHY ARE YOU BUYING LIFE INSURANCE?

According to a story that circulated among conservative evangelical Christians in the 1970s, a denomination that believes strongly in the imminent return of Jesus Christ (which means that it is about to happen) held a ministers' convention at which a guest speaker proclaimed that Jesus is coming soon. The gathered ministers were delighted and ready to go back to their congregations and preach similar sermons. Immediately after the worship service the preachers held a business meeting in which they argued over how their pension funds were being invested by the denomination's headquarters.

This story may be fictional. But its telling played on a felt concern of many reflective Christians even within evangelical circles that purport to believe that Jesus Christ is about to rapture true believers. If that event is so imminent, why be so concerned about the future—especially how money is invested for retirement? (Whether the actual event of the story took place is debatable, but that people who believe in the imminent rapture demonstrate just as much interest in their retirement investments as others is probable. I have witnessed that myself.)

Beliefs about the second coming of Jesus Christ have long been a part of both serious Christian theology and folk Christianity. The first book of academic theology I ever tried to read cover to cover (other than Bible college textbooks) was by a professor of theology at a well-known and highly regarded evangelical Protestant seminary that is noted for promoting belief in the "secret rapture." The author and his seminary are dispensationalists; that is, they interpret Scripture as teaching that the first stage of Christ's return to earth is a secret, invisible departure of authentic Christians to be with Christ in heaven during the so-called "great tribulation," which will last seven years until Christ's public and visible return. Dispensationalists believe that the latter event, known to theologians as the *parousia* (from a Greek word meaning "appearing"), will be followed by one thousand years of Christ ruling and reigning over the earth. This teaching is known as premillennialism. Not all premillennialists believe in a secret rapture; only dispensationalists incorporate that element into their eschatology (doctrine of the end times).

I found the book difficult to read. The prose was turgid and the biblical exegesis was difficult to follow. But above all I found the author's explanations of what will happen in the future speculative and not clearly biblical. It was what I had been taught to believe in the church of my youth, but reading the book helped convince me something was amiss in this scheme of interpreting biblical prophecy. Nevertheless, to this day many serious biblical scholars and theologians have strong arguments for their dispensationalist beliefs. I no longer share them, but I respect them insofar as they are biblically based and reasonable expectations about the future.

POP ESCHATOLOGY AND RAPTURE FEVER

During the 1970s and through the 1990s dispensational beliefs about the future slowly seeped out of academic theology and into folk Christianity through the publication of numerous best-selling Christian books about the end of the world, including the secret rapture and the seven-year great tribulation prior to Christ's second coming. Among the most popular and influential ones were Hal Lindsey's *The Late Great Planet Earth* (Zondervan, 1970) and *Left Behind* by Tim LaHaye and Jerry Jenkins (Tyndale House, 1996). About the time we got married my wife and I attended the world premier of a movie about the rapture and the horrors of the great seven-year tribulation period. *Thief in the Night* was produced by Christians and shown in virtually every fundamentalist and evangelical church in America.

Some people called the phenomenon represented by these books and films "rapture fever." Beliefs about the end times based loosely on biblical apocalyptic literature (Daniel and Revelation) got out of the hands of the theologians and biblical scholars and took on a life of their own with vivid portrayals of the Antichrist and persecutions of Christian believers during the tribulation period.

Evidences of rapture fever in American evangelical folk Christianity included books identifying the year of the rapture (something serious theologians and biblical scholars never do!), movies depicting people suddenly disappearing and others being "left behind" in terror at the rapture, rumors about certain world leaders being the Antichrist based on numerical analyses of their names, and bumper stickers saying, "In case of rapture this car will be driverless." During the 1990s a series of fictional accounts of the rapture and tribulation period were published and became bestsellers even in secular bookstores. Full-length feature films were produced based on the books and dispensationalism entered the mainstream of American society. Even as rapture fever died down, apocalyptic folk religion (as opposed to serious theological treatments of the end times) became the accepted, standard account of Christian eschatology in much of American church life.

What do I mean by "apocalyptic folk religion" and how is that different from serious theological treatments of the biblical materials about the end times? No doubt the line is somewhat difficult to draw. But let me take a stab at it. Apocalyptic folk religion has little to do with serious biblical interpretation and everything to do with symbols that evoke feelings of fear and dread. It is extremely speculative based on fictionalized versions of the future that purport to be based on the Bible but more often than not blend in prominently the author's own personal visions of what the future might be like.

> MUCH of this popular eschatology has little to do with anything the Bible really says about the future. Gradually many evangelical Christians became unaware that the Scripture passages about the future can be interpreted in different ways.

Apocalyptic folk religion thrives on slogans that fit on bumper stickers and popular Christian songs that have little to do with sound biblical interpretation. During the Jesus movement of the early 1970s one popular Jesus freak wrote a song about how horrible it will be to be left behind after the rapture. Together with the movie I mentioned above, the song created a profound sense of fear and dread among many evangelical Christians. Much of this popular eschatology has little to do with anything the Bible really says about the future. Gradually many evangelical Christians became unaware that the Scripture passages about the future can be interpreted in different ways.

Reflective Christianity applies a little critical thought to these matters and asks whether popular images and expectations about the future are really rooted in reasonable interpretations of the Bible or whether they are based on someone's imagination. Serious Bible-believing theologians and biblical scholars may agree with the basic contours of expectation about the future found in apocalyptic folk religion, but they tend to be more modest about the details and they go out of their way to emphasize the symbolic nature of the Bible's apocalyptic literature.

They acknowledge that we will likely be surprised by how things turn out and that the main point of Scripture's teaching about the future is hope rather than fear — especially for believers. They strictly eschew date-setting or making predications about who the Antichrist will be. They know full well that equally devout Christian minds have disagreed for two thousand years about the events of the future surrounding Christ's second coming. And they caution Christians caught up in rapture fever (or simply fascination with the end times) that there are more important subjects for devout attention.

Belief in the return of Jesus Christ to earth is an important part of Christianity; it should not be minimized or ridiculed. The very earliest Christians (after the apostles) wrote about it and used it to encourage persecuted believers. That Christ will return in glory and power to vindicate God's righteousness and to establish peace and justice is a crucial Christian doctrine. Any church that denies it can hardly be called Christian.

Some evangelical churches neglect this doctrine without explicitly denying it. They overreact to rapture fever by downplaying the great biblical truths of hope about the future. In some cases evangelical Christians have become so "at ease in Zion" (old Christian language for affluent and comfortable Christianity) that they are uncomfortable with biblical prophecy that challenges easy accommodation to the present world order. I welcome a revival of interest in future hope among Christians of all stripes; it cannot help but create a certain dis-ease with the present state of the world. Every evangelical church should hear at least one good sermon every year on the second coming of Christ, including resurrection, judgment, and a new heaven and new earth.

> **EVERY** evangelical church should hear at least one good sermon every year on the second coming of Christ, including resurrection, judgment, and a new heaven and new earth.

IS JESUS COMING SOON?

Confessing the "blessed hope" of believers in Christ's return is far different, however, from rapture fever and apocalyptic folk religion. One telltale sign of folk religion is its unexamined nature. Folk religion, including folk Christianity, resists critical thinking and thrives on blind faith in clichés, slogans, snippets of songs and devotional writings, pious novels and movies, Sunday school and youth group teachings, rumors, and evangelegends. To be frank, this blind faith is the basis for much popular evangelical belief about the future.

Some Christians are sure that when the rapture happens, they will suddenly disappear from sight, leaving their unbelieving friends and loved ones bewildered. Some think their clothes and eyeglasses (also false teeth?) will drop from their bodies as they invisibly ascend to be with Christ. Many are convinced it will happen at the least expected moment (which is why they should not be caught in a movie theater watching a PG–13 or R-rated movie!). They tend to believe it will happen like a "thief in the night" even for true Christian believers. This fear has been the basis of many a youth pastor's or youth evangelist's sermon about why daily repentance and obedience are important.

But does the Bible really teach these things? Can many folk Christian beliefs about the future stand up under careful scrutiny? If not, at best they should be relegated to the status of private speculations or at worst rejected by the body of Christ. Let's take a careful and critical look at some of the most popular evangelical beliefs about the future and see if they can withstand examination, using the Bible as our primary source and norm and reason as a necessary tool of interpretation.

The title of this chapter is a common evangelical saying—- "Jesus is coming soon." Popular Christian songs have proclaimed it; numerous evangelical sermons have promoted it. It is probably safe to say most evangelical Christians believe it. But what about the Bible? Does the Bible teach the imminent second coming of

Christ? Are all the prophecies of events leading up to it already fulfilled? Will it be like a thief in the night for Christians—happening when it is least expected? Admittedly, some New Testament passages point toward this. But other clear passages deny it. Unfortunately, many evangelical believers have never had these pointed out to them.

When I want clear biblical teaching about the future, I turn first to Paul's letters rather than to apocalyptic literature such as Daniel and Revelation. That's because the latter speak in symbols that are difficult to interpret. It's as if they are written in code. Christians have never been able to decipher the code perfectly so that all can agree on what the symbols mean. Perhaps as the events begin to happen, people will be able to match the symbols with the realities more closely and clearly. Paul's two letters to the Thessalonians contain much clear and direct teaching about the events surrounding the Lord's second coming.

In 1 Thessalonians 5 the apostle addresses Christians' concerns about "the times and dates" related to the eschaton. It will come "like a thief in the night" (verse 2) and like "labor pains on a pregnant woman" (verse 3). Preachers of the imminence of Christ's coming have pounced on these two verses vigorously and used them to frighten Christians into holy living. While there's nothing wrong with holy living (of course), one has to wonder why the next few verses of the chapter are so often neglected: "But you, brothers and sisters, are not in darkness so that this day should surprise you like a thief. You are all children of the light and children of the day" (verses 4–5).

Similarly, in his "little apocalypse" (often called the Olivet Discourse) Jesus gave his followers signs to look for so that they (and we) would know when he is about to return. Indeed, Jesus also said that even he did not know the "day or hour" of his own return (Matthew 24:36). But in light of his own predictions of events leading up to it, we can only assume that he expected true believers to be prepared, knowing that it is about to happen. Paul shared that assumption with Jesus.

What signs did Jesus and Paul give early Christian believers and us? What should we be looking for so that we can know when he is about to return? One such sign stands out in both Jesus' teachings about this matter and Paul's—the sign of the "abomination that causes desolation" prophesied by Daniel (Matthew 24:15). In 2 Thessalonians 2 Paul reveals clearly what this will be—the revealing of the "man of lawlessness," who will take his seat in the temple of God proclaiming himself to be God and demanding worship. Paul adamantly states that this must come first and afterward "the coming of our Lord Jesus Christ and our being gathered to him" (2:1). The entire second chapter of 2 Thessalonians is about the "signs of the times" that Christians will see that will portend Christ's return. And in the first verse Paul identifies that return as "our being gathered to meet him." That's what people mean by the "rapture" (a word not used in the Bible in any eschatological passage). In other words, whatever the exact nature of the rapture (visible or invisible, public or secret), it will only happen *after* the man of lawlessness (Antichrist) is revealed in that way.

What might Jesus or Paul say to people today who proclaim Christ's imminent return? I think they would say "not yet." The one prophecy that has not yet been fulfilled is the "abomination that causes desolation." We don't even know yet (when this is being written in 2005) who the Antichrist will be! How can the rapture or Christ's *parousia* happen tomorrow? Apparently it can't. And when it does happen, it won't be like a thief in the night except to unbelievers; true followers of Jesus Christ will see the signs of the times and know that their Lord is about to return.

> **THE** *parousia*, the return of Jesus, is always impending and encroaching on our day-to-day lives. It is ever right before us demanding decision and holy living.

Does this mean that all teaching and preaching about the imminence of Christ's return must stop? Not necessarily. But it should make clear that by "imminent" we do not mean "might happen today or tomorrow." Rather, we mean that the *parousia*, the return of Jesus, is always impending and encroaching on our day-to-day lives. It is ever right before us demanding decision and holy living. It may be far off chronologically (clock time) but it is never far off in terms of *kairos*—the time of conversion and transformation. As Christians we are to live with our faces toward the future, living our temporal lives in the light of eternity, which is not mere endlessness of time but God's holy presence.

Christ's coming again is existentially in our immediate future whatever its date may be. We are to keep it in view and let go of attachment to earthly possessions and achievements knowing that our true home is with him. Also, the imminence of Christ's return speaks to us of our own uncertainty of death. Not very long ago a good friend of mine died in his sleep at age fifty-five, which is not really very old. In many ways he was in his prime—especially career-wise. None of us knows the time of our own death and therefore Christ's coming for us is always imminent.

PROBLEMS WITH THE "SECRET RAPTURE"

Another belief that needs careful scrutiny is the so-called "secret rapture." Will Christ's return to earth be public and very noisy, or will it be stealthy and furtive? Some say both. Dispensationalist writers urge Christians to believe that Christ's return will have two stages—one secret and the other (seven years later) very public. The secret stage is the rapture when true believers will be caught up in the air to meet the Lord while others are left to wonder where they went. The public stage is after the seven years of great tribulation when God's wrath is poured out on the earth as the Antichrist battles God's people (the Jews) and is eventually destroyed by the Lord upon his return.

But is this two-stage scheme of the *parousia* biblical? Where does the Bible clearly and unequivocally teach a secret rapture of God's Gentile people, the church? I was raised to believe in it, but when I went to the Bible looking for it, I came up empty handed. I couldn't find it there. In fact, I found clear evidence that Jesus and the New Testament writers thought otherwise. In 2 Thessalonians 2

Paul equates "the coming of our Lord Jesus Christ" and "our being gathered to him." Surely the latter refers to the rapture. But in verse 3 (as noted above) the apostle says, "That day will not come until the rebellion occurs," and he goes on to explain that by "the rebellion" he means what Jesus called the "abomination that causes desolation." So the rapture, whatever exactly it looks like, will not happen until the end of the great tribulation.

How did Paul describe the second coming of Christ? In 1 Thessalonians 4:16–17 Paul describes it this way: "For the Lord himself will come down from heaven, with a loud command, with the voice of the archangel and with the trumpet call of God, and the dead in Christ will rise first. After that, we who are still alive and are left will be caught up together with them in the clouds to meet the Lord in the air." Does this sound like a secret rapture? Hardly. Notice that Paul has to be talking about the rapture because he refers to the resurrection of the dead in Christ, which all dispensationalist writers believe will happen at the rapture. Also, he refers to himself as someone who will possibly be alive being caught up to meet the Lord. Paul's description of the *parousia* here, like other New Testament witnesses elsewhere, assumes it will be a very public, loud event witnessed by everyone. There is no hint of a stealth rapture.

But what about that strange passage in Matthew 24 about one person being taken and the other person being left (24:36–44)? Doesn't that refer to the rapture? First, notice that Jesus nowhere describes this as secret such that the person not raptured is left wondering where the other one went. His comparison is to the days of Noah's flood in the Old Testament, and that was hardly secret or mysterious! Those not in the ark are pounding on it as the rain falls, demanding admission. But also, there's no indication in Jesus' teaching here or elsewhere that the ones "taken" are taken up into a rapture and the ones "left" are left behind to suffer God's wrath. The ones "taken" may very well be swept away in the flood of events of the great tribulation and the ones "left" may very well be the "left behind" to enter God's great kingdom when Christ returns!

TAKING HISTORY SERIOUSLY

So far I've raised questions about popular evangelical beliefs about the imminence and secrecy of Christ's second coming (or certain features of it). I labor under no illusion that I've destroyed these beliefs. That is not my purpose, and even if it were I doubt I could accomplish that. These ideas are too deeply ingrained in the popular Christian mind. All I want to do is persuade Christians to think critically about unexamined assumptions in this matter as in others.

One realization that brought me up short and made me wrestle with the dispensationalist faith of my childhood and youth was that belief in the secret rapture is relatively new as far as Christian history goes. Somehow I had simply assumed that since most of my loved ones, friends, and spiritual mentors believed in it, it had an ancient pedigree and could be found at least here and there throughout church history. That turned out not to be the case. I was surprised to read, for example, that no Christian thought of a secret rapture before the early nineteenth century. My first reaction was, "You mean none of the Reformers of the church knew this?" Then I began to scratch my head in dismay because I didn't see how it was possible for great Christian minds to miss it if it was so clearly taught in Scripture as I had been told. Then I went looking for the idea in the Bible with fresh eyes and couldn't find it there.

Reflective faith cares about history. That's not to say that no new idea can be true. I once heard a Christian speaker say, "If it's new, it can't be true; if it's true, it can't be new." I didn't believe that then and I don't believe that now. God does have new light to break forth from his Word. Luther's great discovery

> **REFLECTIVE** faith cares about history.

of the truth that salvation is by grace through faith alone and does not depend at all on good works or spiritual performance was new. I don't find it in the church fathers or medieval theologians. Still, once Luther pointed it out, millions of Christians saw it in the New Testament. Their eyes had been blinded by tradition.

But can belief in the secret rapture be compared with Luther's wonderful rediscovery of the gospel? I don't think so. So how did the idea of a secret rapture come about? According to historian Dave MacPherson in his book *The Incredible Cover-Up* (Logos, 1975), the first person to teach it based it not on Scripture but on a private revelation she received. This took place in Scotland in 1830; the woman's name was Margaret Macdonald. She prophesied the secret rapture, which was later picked up by her church, Edward Irving's Catholic Apostolic Church (a forerunner of modern Pentecostalism). From there it spread to other evangelical denominations, such as the Plymouth Brethren. From these humble beginnings the doctrine eventually became virtually orthodox among wide swaths of evangelicalism in Europe and North America.

In my folk Christian stage I didn't care about history. By the time I read MacPherson's book with its heavy documentation and looked into the matter for myself, I did care about it. My own inclination toward developing a reasonable faith made me question the importance of a doctrine that began with a private revelation rather recently and bore so little biblical support. Eventually I gave up the belief in a secret rapture and with it most of dispensationalism. I retained my belief in the visible and public return of Christ and the millennium—that Christ will rule and reign on earth for a thousand years—because I found them supported in Scripture (Zechariah 14 and Revelation 20) and the early church fathers (Justin Martyr, Irenaeus, and Tertullian). Nothing of real importance in my Christian faith was lost in the process.

> **REFLECTIVE,** examined, mature faith requires a sifting process where unexamined assumptions are placed under the microscopes of Scripture, tradition, and reason and either established as valid, or revised, or thrown out altogether.

I don't think people have to agree with me to become reflective Christians. But reflective, examined, mature faith requires a sifting process where unexamined assumptions are placed under the microscopes of Scripture, tradition, and reason and either established as valid, or revised, or thrown out altogether.

TAKING IT ALL SERIOUSLY WITHOUT TAKING IT ALL LITERALLY

Let's return to the cliché in this chapter's title. "Jesus is coming soon." True or false? The purpose of this chapter is not to answer that question but to challenge readers to think about the matter critically. And not only should that one issue be subjected to critical examination; the whole web of folk religious ideas about the end times should be brought under scrutiny. What survives as biblically sound and faithful to the best of Christian tradition and reason ought to be held onto firmly. What appears weakly supported by the Bible, reason, and Christian tradition should be questioned and at best placed in the category of speculation. The whole phenomenon of rapture fever should calm down, and people caught up in it should settle for the stable teaching of the Bible about the future. The biblical story of the future is meant to encourage and give hope; it is not meant to fuel speculation, fear, or inordinate fascination.

THE biblical story of the future is meant to encourage and give hope; it is not meant to fuel speculation, fear, or inordinate fascination.

So, inquiring minds want to know—is Jesus coming soon? Yes and no. The first Christians apparently believed in the imminent return of their Lord. And with good reason. The second to last verse of the Bible quotes Jesus saying, "I am coming soon" (Revelation 22:20). Paul thought he might live to see that day. He certainly thought some of his converts would be alive when the Lord returned. He was wrong about that. Nevertheless, the early Christians were not entirely wrong. They lived lives of hopeful expectation and experienced the breaking in of God's glorious kingdom even though its fullness was at least two thousand years away as clocks and calendars keep time.

Let me offer a homely analogy to explain my yes and no answer. Suppose a dear and famous friend in a distant place writes to tell you she is coming to visit and says "very soon" but does not give a definite time. Her letter mentions some signs that will precede her arrival, including delivery of some of her luggage in stages—first a small suitcase and then a large trunk. But no definite date is communicated. You immediately begin anticipating her visit with excitement and tell all your friends that your famous friend is about to visit you. You don't know exactly when, but it will happen "soon." But times goes on and nothing arrives. You know your friend well enough to believe she is coming, so you keep on making preparations so that whenever it happens you'll be ready. You live your day-to-day life in the light of this great and exciting event.

One day someone says to you, "I discovered your famous friend is arriving tomorrow. Let's go down to the airport and sit there and wait for her." What would be your response? "No, none of her luggage has arrived yet—not even her small suitcase. But I'm looking for her soon and striving to be ready for her." "Soon" does not mean "tomorrow." It may be a ways off in chronological time. But your daily expectation and readiness makes her arrival "soon" whenever it will happen.

Even though I believe Jesus cannot come back "tomorrow" (as of October 5, 2005) because his "luggage" (portents of his coming) has not yet arrived, I watch hopefully and expectantly for his appearing so as not to be caught "asleep" like those who have no hope (1 Thessalonians 5:6). My faith in Jesus' return is not all that different in content from its childhood form; now as then I believe in and watch for Christ's return.

> I live my temporal life in eternity's light and regard every day and moment as the one right before my Lord returns because it is a day and moment of decision to be for or against his lordship.

The difference is that it is no longer childish; I now know more time will pass as prophesied events unfold and that the day and hour of his return cannot be predicted. I live my temporal life in eternity's light and regard every day and moment as the one right before my Lord returns because it is a day and moment of decision to be for or against his lordship.

So, should you buy life insurance if you believe Jesus is coming soon? When asked what he would do if God revealed to him that Jesus would return tomorrow, Martin Luther said he would plant a tree. In other words, we are called to occupy the world in which God has placed us whatever will happen tomorrow. It is always a good time to do the good. But if I were convinced that Jesus' return is imminent in the sense many people mean (tomorrow or the next day), I would not buy life insurance. The mere fact that they do raises a question mark over the sincerity or intensity of their belief. But since I do not know the "when" of Christ's "soon" return, I do buy life insurance—and plant trees and look forward to retirement and plan next semester's classes.

DISCUSSION QUESTIONS

1. What beliefs have you held about the return of Jesus Christ? Have you believed it is imminent? What about the "secret rapture"? Where did you get these beliefs?

2. Do you agree that many popular ideas and images of Christ's return derive more from fiction and imagination than from Scripture? What are some examples besides those mentioned in the chapter?

3. Do you agree that every church should hear at least one sermon annually about the second coming of Jesus Christ? Why? Does your church hear that? If not, why do you think that is the case?

4. After reading this chapter do you have questions or concerns about the beliefs regarding the future that you held before reading it? Where has the chapter raised questions about your beliefs? What do you now (after reading the chapter) believe about the events of the future (with regard to Christ's return)?

5. Why should evangelical Christians take history very seriously? If a doctrine or teaching is absent from most of Christian history, is that a mark against it? How can Christian history help you when you come across new or unfamiliar teachings?

6. What do you think about this chapter's account of the meaning of the "imminence" of Christ's return? Can it be truly imminent and yet possibly far off in the future?

CHAPTER 8

ALL SINS ARE EQUAL:

SO IS REUSING A STAMP AS BAD AS MURDER?

Some questions are designed simply to make us think. The question in this chapter's title is just such a question. It's tongue-in-cheek; it isn't totally serious. But it is aimed straight at the heart of folk Christianity because it provokes critical thinking and reflection about a commonly believed and repeated evangelical cliché: "All sins are equal, you know." I can't begin to estimate how many times I've heard it said in theology classes, in common spaces of Christian colleges and universities, in churches, and everywhere evangelical Christians gather and talk. "All sins are equal, you know." Is that true?

I've hardly ever heard this maxim questioned. Most people to whom it is said nod in agreement. That is, unless they're Catholics. That sins are not equal is part of Catholic doctrine. This particular saying is especially popular among Protestants probably in reaction against the Catholic distinction between mortal and venial sins and even among venial sins. A mortal sin is one that cuts a person off from God; the only response to having committed a mortal sin is specific remorse and repentance, including some kind of penitential activity. A venial sin is one that should be confessed to a priest but does not automatically break fellowship with God. If it goes without repentance, it can erode a person's spiritual life, but by itself it won't cause a person to be condemned.

The Protestant Reformation of the sixteenth century was a valid reaction against abuses within the Catholic church and a helpful and necessary correction of its false teachings. Martin Luther and John Calvin, along with other Reformers, rejected the Catholic penitential system, including the distinction between mortal and venial sins. For them, sin is much deeper than outward acts of disobedience; it is a wrong attitude toward God and toward other people that lies in the heart, at the root of all sinful acts. It is also a fundamental spiritual disability to please God because of pride and selfishness. They called it total depravity not because it makes people as bad as they possibly can be but because it infects every corner of the human personality and leaves no aspect of humanity clean and pure.

The Reformers believed that the Catholic theology of their time did not take sin seriously enough; it implied to average priests and lay Catholics that only a few sins break off our relationship with God and as long as we avoid those, go to confession, and perfunctorily perform penitential acts assigned by the priest, all will eventually be well. Whether this is good Catholic theology is another question. But it was the widespread impression among Catholics in the sixteenth century.

REASONS FOR THIS BELIEF (AND WHY THEY ARE NOT VALID)

Nowhere did either Luther or Calvin or any of the other Protestant Reformers say that all sins are equal, but that impression caught on among Protestant laypeople and now has the status of a virtual item of Protestant orthodoxy. To challenge it is to go against so much that so many evangelical Christians hold dear. I've raised questions about it among my students numerous times and every time the reaction is the same—utter surprise and some dismay. Those who are knowledgeable about Catholic theology want to know if I also believe in purgatory! That's quite a leap! Others just want me to explain myself. I'm immediately on the defensive. All their lives they've heard that all sins are equal. Some will cautiously clarify it with "in God's sight," which is better. It's shocking to them to hear their theology professor challenge what they take for granted as a biblical truth.

I've asked students why they believe all sins are equal—beyond the mere fact that they've been told it. I ask them where the Bible says it and whether it is reasonable in light of the hideous variety of evils in the world. One reason they believe all sins are equal is that to say otherwise raises the question of who determines which sins are more serious than others and on what grounds. My response is that just because we don't know which sins are more serious than others doesn't mean there aren't any.

Suppose I move to a foreign country and don't know the laws of the road at all. If I'm going to drive, I should do my best to find out what they are. But just because I don't know whether speeding or running a red light is more serious doesn't mean one isn't worse. This is the difference between the "order of knowing" and the "order of being"—a distinction too little known or understood by most people. It is one thing not to know something; it is quite another thing for that something not to exist. There are many things that are real that I don't know or understand. My not knowing or understanding doesn't mean they don't exist.

But the response also assumes that in order for there to be degrees of sinfulness among sins there has to be some human judge who decides which sins are more serious than others. Even in the foreign country where I drive without knowing the rules of the road someone knows them, and if I'm taken to court for violating them a judge will gladly tell me how serious my violations were. But suppose we're not talking about laws but about social norms.

I've lived in a different country and experienced culture shock. A big part of culture shock is not knowing what is expected of one's self in certain situations. For example, in some parts of Germany Sunday is a "quiet day" and people are expected to respect their neighbors by not making noise. They take that seriously. Anyone who throws open his windows and lets loud music blare will be shunned by neighbors and possibly confronted by them as well. That's true even if the traffic on the street is quite loud. We were visiting a medieval town with walls and turrets on a Sunday afternoon. Many people were there for a festival. We stood on a sidewalk and enjoyed the sights and sounds of a large boys' band as it marched down the main street. People were waving out their windows and thoroughly enjoying the "oompahpah" music so traditional in that part of Germany.

After the boys' band marched out of sight and hearing, our four-year-old daughter wanted to ride on a little coin-operated merry-go-round on the sidewalk. So we put a coin in it and she laughed and sang as it went around. A little old German lady came up to us and scolded us for allowing our daughter to make noise on Sunday! Needless to say, we found that funny. After all, a very noisy boys' band had just gone by. But that's our American perspective. In that part of Germany a noisy festival on a Sunday afternoon is one thing; a child laughing and singing loudly on a now quiet street is something else altogether. We experienced such dissonances often as we tried to navigate our experience of German culture and its differences from American culture. The point is that some lapses are more serious than others even in the absence of any authority to delineate the distinctions precisely. Some tear at the social fabric more than others.

Another defense of the cliché that all sins are equal is that once we start recognizing a hierarchy of sins, we give license to some people to feel "holier than thou" toward other people. And the Bible says we all sin. Yes, it does. But it doesn't say all sins are equal. Still, I want to take this objection seriously. Does acknowledging that some sins are worse than others lead to a hierarchy of sins and then to pride because one hasn't committed the more awful sins? Perhaps—but not necessarily. I can turn the tables and ask whether leveling all sins so that none is more serious than others leads to a slack attitude toward and treatment of sin. (More on that later.) That some sins are worse than others gives no ground to pride because, as the Bible says, we are all sinners.

Suppose I make it through one day without committing any overt act of sin. Maybe I slept the whole day because I was sick. (That's about the only kind of day I could go through without sinning!) Does that mean I had a "sinless day"? I'm raising the issue of "sin" versus "sins." According to Christian theology sin is not just outward acts but even more an inward disposition. Jesus taught that hate is as murder and Paul taught that love of money is the root of all kinds of evil (1 Timothy 6:10). The witness of the New Testament about sin is that it is a fundamental disposition of the heart that sets itself against God. Most Christian theologians (especially Protestants) identify sin as self-idolatry or refusal of creatureliness. Adam and Eve sinned because of a basic attitude of distrust toward God and desire to be as God for themselves. Their actual eating of the fruit of the tree was the result of a sinful disposition.

So, on that mythical day when I committed no sins I was still a sinner, because sin lies in the core or center of my personality. That's the human condition according to the Bible and Protestant theology. I should repent every day even if I can't think of a single overt, presumptuous sin I committed, because

> **ACCORDING** to Christian theology sin is not just outward acts but even more an inward disposition.

some aspect of my very personhood is set against God. Therefore, even if I manage to make it through one day without overtly sinning, I still have no basis for pride for the root of sin is still within me. I don't have to feel it to sense it. And the Bible reveals that root. (I take Romans 7 to be Paul's account of the normal Christian life rather than his description of his pre-Christian existence. We are all like Paul in the struggle between fallen nature and the Holy Spirit who dwells in us and calls us to higher things.)

Thus, recognizing a hierarchy of sins does nothing to detract from everyone's sinfulness. Our basic problem is not that we commit sins; it is that we are born sinners and will be that way until we are glorified in heaven. We may be forgiven sinners, but we are sinners nevertheless.

ALL SINS CANNOT BE EQUAL

I hope I have overcome some of the objections to my challenge to the belief that all sins are equal. But why challenge it? What harm does it do? Why not just let people think and say that all sins are equal? Can that be disproved? Why is it considered folk Christianity?

That's a lot of questions and the tables are now turned on me! I ought to examine my own belief about this and not assume I am right. Critical thinking about assumptions is always a good and helpful thing. For one thing, common sense seems to go against the idea that all sins are equal. It's one thing to say we are all equally sinners. With that I can agree because, as I've explained, Christian theology says we are all born sinners because of Adam and Eve. From them we inherit "original sin" and total depravity. (Original sin is inherited condemnation because sinner Adam is our moral and spiritual "head" according to Paul in Romans 5; total depravity is our inherited condition of being naturally inclined toward sin and away from God.) The guilt of original sin is taken away by the cross of Jesus Christ (Romans 5), but our bent toward sinning remains and lures us into sins. I don't think anyone totally escapes that condition. So we are all equally sinners in that sense of sharing together and equally in the fallen human condition.

But common sense tells me that some people embrace their fallenness and act it out in more radical and damaging ways than others. Are we to say that Hitler was no worse than the poor wretch who steals a loaf of bread because he and his family are hungry?

What about murderers and petty thieves? Are their sins equal even before God? We all agree that their crimes are not equal, but what about their sins?

When I was a child my stepmother suffered from what some theologians call scrupulosity. She carefully weighed and examined every little action to see whether it was sinful. She lived in a black and white world where everything was either a sin or not a sin, and she felt it was her duty to determine that for herself and us boys. I remember one day a letter came to our house with a stamp not cancelled (postmarked) by the post office. There was not a mark on it; the stamp was pristine. My father (who was a minister) planned to remove the stamp and use it. We were pretty poor. To him this was a godsend. God was providing in another little way; the little ways added up. But my stepmother's scrupulosity kicked in and ruined the stamp so it could not be reused, declaring that it would be theft against the U.S. government to reuse it. The fact that it was not postmarked was a mistake; we should treat it as if it were cancelled.

> SOME people embrace their fallenness and act it out in more radical and damaging ways than others.

I remember thinking she was right but made too big a deal out of the matter. Would it have been a sin to carefully remove the stamp and reuse it? Might it be the case that God was providing for us? How was this really different from finding money (which happened rarely but occasionally and always brought great rejoicing to our household!)? I've never really settled the matter in my mind. It seems trivial, but I remember it because it became the occasion of much theological discussion in our little family. Now I ask whether a person who says that all sins are equal would say that reusing a stamp accidentally not cancelled by the post office is as much a sin as murdering the postal worker who delivered it? I can't imagine anyone seriously thinking that. The cliché sounds nice when uttered against scholastic distinctions between mortal and venial sins, but can it really hold up under scrutiny? I think common sense weighs in against that.

Of course, someone might respond that the whole cliché is that all sins are equal "in God's sight." Slogans have a way of getting abbreviated over time. Often that process makes them more tenuous and less tenable. Let's say the whole saying is, "All sins are equal in God's sight." That's better. Maybe. Let's subject it to critical examination. What it adds to "All sins are equal" is a qualifier—- "in God's sight." In other words, they are not equal in terms of human judgment, but they all equally alienate us from God and God from us. They are equally damaging to our relationship with God. Or, they all equally call for repentance because without that they all equally bring condemnation. This means that murder is not equal with petty thievery in a human court; the former brings a harsher sentence than the latter.

We generally recognize and support the distinction between felonies and misdemeanors. But according to this more complete version of the slogan, murder and petty theft (such as shoplifting) equally break our relationship with God. In God's sight both equally call for judgment and condemnation. Or, in softer terms, both equally hurt God and cause him grief.

Adding "in God's sight" helps. But I don't think it rescues the saying from criticism. I'll just lay all my cards on the table and admit it right now: I think the cliché that all sins are equal (even only in God's sight) is folk religion and not sound theology. My hypothesis is that it arises from two sources. First, it was first coined as a Protestant protest against the Catholic hierarchy of sins. Second, it is sustained by a desire not to have to deal with sin in ourselves or in others.

The first reason for saying this cliché ought to be rejected. We shouldn't believe things just because someone else believes differently. I once asked a group of Baptist students why the Baptist churches in their southern state generally celebrate the Lord's Supper only once a quarter (if that often). Their response was,

> TOO often we do or don't do certain things simply to mark boundaries between our own tribe and someone else's. That's bad theologically.

"Because we don't want to be like the Churches of Christ that celebrate it every Sunday." Too often we do or don't do certain things simply to mark boundaries between our own tribe and someone else's. That's bad theologically. Whenever we discover that this is the only or primary reason for a belief or practice, we should toss it out or revise it.

The second reason is even worse. I suspect that the reason people claim that all sins are equal is so they don't have to do anything about sin in their own lives (other than repent to God) or in the lives of other Christians.

ESPECIALLY BAD SINS AND TOUGH LOVE

The context in which the slogan is uttered is revealing. That's usually a discussion of a revelation about some Christian leader's fall from grace because of a sexual affair or a financial scandal. Or it may just be a discussion of a friend's or acquaintance's besetting sin that recently came to light. For example, a group of students are sitting around talking about a fellow student who admitted to a pornography addiction during a spiritual small group time. (This is much more common than many people want to think!) Then someone says, "Yes, that's too bad. But you know, all sins are equal, so it's between him and God." What does that really mean? What's the performance of the utterance (to use philosophical language)? It means, "So let's not confront him or hold him accountable or do anything else about this."

Far be it from me to decide what always ought to be done in such a situation. But I suspect the cliché is what philosophers call a "speech act," which has the effect of advocating a hands-off approach to the poor young man who needs help. What kind of help does he need? Probably intervention and accountability from caring but firm friends. Tough love. What if a young woman in the same spiritual group confessed to occasionally lusting after Brad Pitt? People would probably laugh and say, "That's normal. But we'll pray and ask God to help you with this." What if a young man in the group confessed to murdering his parents? Would anyone say, "All sins are equal"? Of course not. In that case they would probably take the matter to authorities.

Short of crimes, however, modern evangelicals are loathe to intervene in others' lives even when they need it desperately and even when their sin could cause great harm within the body of Christ. Belief that all sins are equal can serve as a support to this aversion; it can justify nonintervention in cases of egregious sin within the church and among Christians. The New Testament, however, gives us examples of intervention and even exclusion in some cases of ongoing sin among Christians. It also plainly refutes the idea that all sins are equal—even in God's sight.

> **SHORT** of crimes, however, modern evangelicals are loathe to intervene in others' lives even when they need it desperately and even when their sin could cause great harm within the body of Christ.

Let's begin with the example of church discipline. In 1 Corinthians 5 Paul orders his Corinthian converts to exclude one of their own from the church because he was living in an adulterous and perhaps incestuous relationship with his father's wife (the Greek makes it difficult to know the exact relationship between the man and the woman). The man, he says, is to be put out of the fellowship and handed over to Satan. That's pretty harsh. Surely everyone sinned in some way. This was a particularly heinous sin that had to be dealt with openly and harshly.

That example from the New Testament pretty much undermines the idea that all sins are equal. They certainly weren't to Paul. Some called for harsh measures toward the sinners; others apparently did not. Paul didn't say, "O well, all sins are equal, you know." He said, "There is sexual immorality among you, and of a kind that even pagans do not tolerate" (1 Corinthians 5:1). He was clearly shocked and dismayed. Would he have reacted similarly had he known some of the Corinthian Christians were gossiping or overeating? Apparently not. Surely they were. Paul was never soft on sin, but some sins provoked particularly strong words of condemnation. What would Paul have thought of our laissez-faire attitude of "All sins are equal"? I'm sure he would have disapproved.

Also in 1 Corinthians Paul singles out one particular sin as especially bad. In Greek it is *porneia*—translated into English as "immorality." *Porneia* is a catch-all word for all kinds of sexual deviance and immorality. Paul treats it as especially evil and harmful. In chapter 6 he singles out *porneia* and says, "Flee from sexual immorality. All other sins a man commits are outside his body, but he who sins sexually sins against his own body. Do you not know that your body is a temple of the Holy Spirit, who is in you, whom you have received from God?" (verses 18–19 NIV). We usually interpret "body" here (as elsewhere) as referring to the individual's own physical frame, but it's possible Paul is referring to the body of Christ. Otherwise it is difficult to understand his logic here.

If "body" in 1 Corinthians 6:18–19 refers to the church, however, Paul's ire against immorality makes sense. He is especially worked up about pagan temple prostitution, which was common in the Roman world; some of the Corinthian Christians were apparently continuing to engage in it even after accepting Christ. Paul's argument is that this kind of immorality is idolatrous as well as immoral and constitutes a sin against the Spirit of God, who indwells and unites the church with Christ. Whatever exactly Paul has in mind in this case, one thing is clear: he does have a hierarchy of sins in his own mind. This one, whatever exactly it is (whether temple prostitution per se or any immorality), is particularly evil.

EQUALITY OF SINFULNESS AND HIERARCHY OF SINS

So what should we conclude about degrees of sin? Could it be that Catholic and Protestant theologies are both partly right? Is it possible that all sins are equal and yet there exists a hierarchy of sins? To me, this both-and approach makes more sense than the either-or approach. Catholic theology makes too much of the distinction between mortal and venial sins. Protestant theology (especially in its folk religious expression) makes too much of the equality of sins. Surely it is reasonable to conclude that all sins contribute to alienation from God and grieve the heart of God.

No sin is trivial since it offends God's holiness and righteousness and tears at the fabric of our humanity and our relationship with God. Even reusing a stamp mistakenly not cancelled at the post office can damage one's intimacy with God and incur God's disciplining wrath especially if it goes against conscience. To call any sin "venial" implies that it is trivial. Sin is never trivial. However, it also trivializes heinous sins to place them on the same plane with reusing a stamp. Some kind of distinction between murder and adultery on the one hand, and petty thievery on the other, must be made in order not to minimize and trivialize the former.

> NO sin is trivial since it offends God's holiness and righteousness and tears at the fabric of our humanity and our relationship with God.

I don't think the right approach is to create categories of sins such as mortal and venial. Nevertheless, some recognition of a hierarchy of sins is needed. That's probably a matter best left to each spiritual community (denomination, church, or religious group). On what grounds? What criteria should be used to distinguish the worse sins from those not as bad? I suggest two criteria. First, some sins more effectively ruin lives than others. Within "lives" I include both the individual's physical, emotional, and mental well-being and one's relationship with God. Apparently, according to Paul, *porneia* (immorality) does that. It tears at the fabric of one's life, including one's spiritual life. It damages character because it is addictive and leads to harmful obsessions that in turn lead to worse sins, such as sexual perversions of all kinds. It distorts and destroys relationships and goes against love.

Second, some sins do greater damage to the church than others. The church's reputation is destroyed by immorality especially among its leaders. It creates division within Christ's body. It sets up an odious atmosphere that blocks the work of the Spirit among the people.

I don't mean to single out immorality as if it were the only particularly noxious sin. Paul also condemns as especially destructive division and strife as well as legalism. In Galatians he sternly warns the Christians there that trying to please God by the law causes one to have "fallen away from grace" (Galatians 5:4). Rarely does Paul mention sins such as gossip or overeating although occasionally he includes them as "works of the flesh." The emphasis he places on certain sins, however, reveals his hierarchy of sins. His logic has to do with the harm the worse sins do to persons and to the body of Christ.

I believe a careful examination of New Testament teaching about sin will lead us to recognize some sins as worse than others while at the same time acknowledging every sin has negative consequences and, if practiced repeatedly without repentance, corrodes one's relationship with God. What's the practical value of this? Just this—only by recognizing a hierarchy of sins will we get back to some practice of church discipline without which everything is tolerated and the body of Christ is dragged down in reputation and moral purity. Certainly we cannot discipline every person for every sin, but we can and must intervene lovingly but firmly in cases of immorality, murder, blasphemy, chronic lying, greed, hatred, and heresy.

The point of this chapter, as every chapter of this book, has not been to attack one particular popular Christian cliché and correct those who utter it. Rather, the purpose has been to illustrate how a widely believed saying can be far off the mark biblically and practically and yet contain a measure of truth. Furthermore, the point here has been to illustrate once again how to examine such an unexamined belief and work toward its reevaluation and revision. Common sense combined with careful biblical interpretation and application serve as the antidote to the poison of folk religion.

COMMON sense combined with careful biblical interpretation and application serve as the antidote to the poison of folk religion.

But the outcome is not a complete dismissal of the cliché as utterly without truth or value. All sin is equal in God's sight insofar as it goes without repentance and expresses an evil disposition of the heart. But some sins are especially destructive of the human person and his or her relationship with God, and some sins are particularly damaging to the church's spiritual health, unity, and reputation. A little faithful and critical thinking leads inexorably to such a conclusion.

DISCUSSION QUESTIONS

1. Have you been taught or concluded on your own that all sins are equal? How were you taught that? Why do you think you were taught that? How did you come to that conclusion on your own?

2. What do you think about the Catholic distinction between mortal and venial sins? Is there some validity to that?

3. Do you agree that too often we arrive at our beliefs in reaction against some other belief system that we want to avoid? Is that a proper way to justify our beliefs? If not, how should we arrive at and justify our beliefs?

4. What do you think about the place of church discipline in contemporary churches? Would you agree that churches in America are too lax when it comes to church discipline so that even extremely damaging sin is ignored or condoned? What consequences can lack of church discipline bring to the church? Does the church need to rediscover church discipline? How might it do that?

5. After reading this chapter what do you think about believing in a hierarchy of sins? If you think that's legitimate,

what sins would you count as particularly awful and which ones would you count as less so? Why?

6. What overall effect has this chapter had on your view of sin? Has it tended to make you take sin more seriously? Or has it tended to trivialize sin for you? Why?

In our postmodern, tolerant society it seems everybody's favorite Bible verse is: "Do not judge, or you too will be judged" (Matthew 7:1). In popular religious parlance this gets translated in all kinds of ways: "Don't judge another until you walk a mile in his shoes"; "Who are you to judge another person? He (or she) has a unique relationship with God"; and "Let God be their judge." As usual, there's lots of truth in all these sayings. It's hard to find a common cliché that is totally devoid of truth; they all seem to contain that essential kernel of truth that gives them their popularity and currency. Certainly God is the ultimate judge of every person's soul; if Matthew 7:1 means any-thing, it must be that God alone decides each one's eternal destiny. We are forbidden to take God's place and pronounce that judgment on anyone. That's why especially conservative Christians forbid saying "Go to hell," even when they're angry at someone. Only God decides on the population of heaven and hell. In that sense we are not other people's judges.

I wonder, however, if there's another reason why this saying (in its various forms) is so popular among Christians and others in contemporary church and society. Could it be another case where culture has taken a precious truth and inflated it to the point of serious distortion? Perhaps we should ask some tough questions about "Judge not" before spouting it in response to someone who makes a value claim about behavior or lifestyle. After all, that's when this slogan usually comes out — in response to a person or group who pronounces a certain behavior sinful.

You can almost count on it if you're in a large group. Someone says that such-and-such a behavior is sinful, and someone else says "Judge not that ye be not judged" (the commonly known King James Version of Matthew 7:1). Is the saying in that context really sound Christian wisdom, or is it folk religion misusing a portion of Jesus' Sermon on the Mount? Too seldom do we ask such ques-tions. We simply hear a nice-sounding cliché and endorse and re-peat it. Some have even vulgarized it to "Who appointed *you* judge of the world?" We ought to question the view that people should never judge one another in light of Scripture, common sense, tradi-tion, reason, and experience. Will it hold up under scrutiny? Is it universally true or only true in certain situations?

TOLERANCE AND AMERICAN CULTURE

It would never enter most evangelical Christians' minds that they are accommodating to their culture when they say "Judge not!" But I submit that is exactly what they are doing — in many cases — not in every case, to be sure, but in some. Sociologists tell us that American culture is radically individualistic. Robert

Bellah, a noted sociologist of religion, argued in *Habits of the Heart* (University of California Press, 1985) that this radical individualism infects religion in strange ways that most religious Americans are not even aware of.

Perhaps it takes living in another culture to notice how individually centered ours is. From early childhood into early adulthood we are bombarded with the message that the highest value, the magnet in our moral compass, ought to be: "Be true to yourself." Self-love, self-esteem, self-actualization all saturate the media and education; we are a nation of individual selves seeking our own identities, often in competition with others and with the common good. We interpret freedom individualistically and sometimes hedonistically as if it could only be fully experienced through experiencing everything possible.

> WE are a nation of individual selves seeking our own identities, often in competition with others and with the common good.

Whenever I hear someone uttering "Judge not" or its equivalent, I wonder to myself what they mean by that. And I wonder if they are saying it to protect individualism—their own and that of others. I suspect that's the real reason why "Judge not" stands out as the only verse in the Bible most people know by heart (even if they can't begin to say where it is found!). They have been influenced by our individualistic culture that so highly values freedom of expression and experience; the worst thing someone can do to another is suppress his or her freedom to express oneself.

One perspective we have adopted to protect this attitude is moral relativism. That's the idea that there are no absolutes of right and wrong; these differ depending on the person and the situation. Along with individualism and relativism comes tolerance as the highest value. In this case, tolerance no longer means putting up with bad behavior but refusing to recognize any behavior as bad (except judging itself!). Of course, most Americans do have their limits of tolerance; it slips away when something precious to them is being taken away or harmed. But in their general mood

QUESTIONS TO ALL YOUR ANSWERS

tolerance governs relations and comes into play against anything that seems to hinder free expression and free experience.

Unfortunately, too many Christians have succumbed to this cultural mood, or at least it has infected their thinking in an unreflective way. What I mean by that is they have unthinkingly adopted some elements of the culture of individualism, relativism, and tolerance into their lives. Many of my Christian college students jump to the "Don't judge" imperative whenever someone makes a claim that certain beliefs or behaviors are simply wrong and ought to be condemned. It is so predictable that it's like pushing a button and waiting for the candy to come out of the machine. We are programmed by our culture to react negatively to whatever sounds judgmental. Gradually that has come to encompass virtually all criticisms of behavior.

But can this be squared with reason, let alone the gospel? Is it really possible to avoid judging? Isn't the declaration, "You're judging and that's bad" (which is implied in most cases where "Judge not!" is uttered), itself judging? This is what philosophers call a self-referentially defeating statement unless it is limited to certain kinds of judging. If all judging is bad, then condemning judging is bad.

Before we get too deep into examining "Judge not!" we should examine the culture that supports this knee-jerk declaration. Christians are called to stand against culture insofar as it contradicts the gospel. We saw in chapter 8 how subversion by the dominant culture can distract Christians from doing the hard work of acknowledging the seriousness of sin in themselves and others and dealing with that. The gospel says we are all sinners and deserving of God's condemnation unless we repent and receive his mercy. The gospel also calls us to accountability to God and to the church. The church is an essential part of the gospel; we can't get away from that. It's all over the New Testament. There is no Lone Ranger Christianity in the Bible; biblical Christianity is thoroughly communal.

It's true, of course, that each individual stands before God alone in repentance and conversion; nobody can repent for another person or be converted for him or her. However, discipleship is something that develops and thrives only within the body of Christ, the church. If you have any doubts about it, read in Paul's letters those parts that emphasize the role of the community of God's people in one's individual relationship with God. We are each part of Christ's own body and we are to function in harmony with all the other parts. Paul even goes so far as to call the church "Christ" (1 Corinthians 12:12). Apparently our relationship with Christ cannot thrive apart from our relationship with the church, which is his presence in the world.

> OUR relationship with Christ cannot thrive apart from our relationship with the church, which is his presence in the world.

All this goes against our highly individualistic culture. At this point, anyway, authentic Christianity must be countercultural. We are individuals, but individualism can be an idolatry of our individuality when we stand over against the community and its common good. Putting aside the gospel for the moment, we might ask whether American individualism even makes sense. If everyone is expected to exert his or her individuality in an extreme way, that individualism becomes a herd mentality. In such a context the real individual would be the person who sacrifices individualism for the common good of the community!

All this is simply to say that while Christians should value the individual as someone uniquely created and gifted by God, we should also seek to harmonize individuality with community. Sacrifice of self for others is the way of the cross, and Paul the apostle urged the early Christians to put aside their rights out of concern for the consciences of weaker believers (1 Corinthians 10:23–30). Such communitarian living also makes sense whereas extreme individualism is ultimately irrational and unworkable.

> WHILE Christians should value the individual as someone uniquely created and gifted by God, we should also seek to harmonize individuality with community.

THE MANY MEANINGS OF "JUDGING"

One problem with "Judge not," then, is that it too often is uttered to protect a cultural way of life that is contrary to the gospel. It can be and often is an expression of American individualism, relativism, and tolerance. Christians should examine what they and others mean by this phrase. If it is merely mouthing popular culture's desire to protect individual freedom of self-assertion and experience of anything and everything even against the common good of the community, it can't be compatible with authentic Christianity. Too often it is merely evidence of accommodation to culture, which is ironic because when Jesus said "Judge not" in Matthew 7:1, he was going against the prevailing culture of his day, which was legalistic and overly judgmental toward individuals.

But another problem with "Judge not!" lies with the terms "judge" and "judging." They are ambiguous. Some judging is unavoidable. Too many people lump all judging together as if it is bad when they themselves make judgments every day. Which fast food is best? Which college is better than others? Which boys or girls are better looking? Which contestant in a contest stands out as making the best performance? In a court of law is the defendant guilty or not? These are all examples of judging that is common, unavoidable, and necessary. We do them all the time without even thinking about it. So, in some senses, "judging" is acknowledged by everyone as having some validity. "Judge not!" cannot apply to all kinds of judging.

When most Christians utter this phrase, they are referring to a particular kind of judging. What kind of judging? First, of course, is the kind I mentioned at the beginning of this chapter — declaring someone's eternal destiny (usually in hell). I believe the directive to "Judge not" is properly aimed at someone who says to or about another person "Go to hell!" (or, "He should go to hell!"). The proper Christian response is a judgment of that attitude and declaration — "Judge not!"

That's what I believe Christ was talking about in Matthew 7:1. He was commanding his followers to avoid usurping God's role in judging people's ultimate and final destiny or even their relationship with God. Whom God accepts as right with him (justified) is his business and not ours. We are not called to be judges of other people's salvation. Students often ask me during the study of modern Christian theology whether I think a certain German theologian who denied the bodily resurrection of Jesus Christ is in heaven right now. (He died in the 1970s.) I decline to reply except by explaining that that is God's business and none of mine.

Often, however, Christians who say "Judge not!" are not provoked by a blatant declaration of another person's unsaved status. They are responding to a statement about some person's or group's status as "not Christian." Or they are responding to a statement about a certain belief or behavior as incompatible with Christianity. For example, in group conversation one Christian says about members of a certain religious tradition that does not consider Jesus as God incarnate, "They're not even Christians, you know." Almost inevitably another person in the group says, "You shouldn't judge them like that." Or in another conversation one Christian says, "People who do that aren't Christians." You can be sure someone else is going to pipe up with "Judge not lest ye be judged." A widespread assumption exists even among Christians that expressing opinions about what is and what is not Christian (or compatible with being Christian) is inappropriate judging.

APPROPRIATE JUDGING

Some years ago I directed a Christian coffeehouse in a small Midwestern city. Most of the denizens were either Jesus freaks or hippies. On Friday and Saturday evenings we held Bible studies after singing contemporary Christian choruses led by long-haired, sandal-wearing, guitar-strumming musicians. (Larry Norman's "I Wish We'd All Been Ready" was a favorite!) A new religious group came to town and established a commune in a large house not far from our coffeehouse. The leaders wore black robes and uniforms that looked vaguely like monks' or priests' garb. They walked the downtown streets at night especially on weekends looking for young people to bring to their commune for their own spiritual studies and meditation sessions. Two of the group's leaders began to hang out at our coffeehouse and tried to recruit Jesus people and seekers to their movement.

I decided to find out what this new sect was all about, but even the local seminary library had no information on them. This was before the internet, so I had to write to some experts on cults and new religions. Very little help came my way. Finally I found two of their books in a local bookstore. I bought them and devoured them, looking for their real teachings, which they seemed to want to hide. I found there what I suspected. They believed in reincarnation, spirit guides (including Jesus, whom they did not consider God incarnate), astrology, and all kinds of mystical and occult ideas and practices. They tried to blend it with Christianity so that their belief system was much like the Gnostics of early Christianity. (Early Christian Gnostics blended extreme forms of Greek religious beliefs and philosophy into their Christianity so that matter, including the body, was denigrated and the incarnation of God in Jesus was considered impossible.)

One evening I taught the Bible study about this group and their real beliefs. The two leaders sat in the front row in their black clerical robes staring at me and taking notes. I told the coffeehouse crowd what I had learned just from reading the books by the sect's leader. They couldn't challenge what I said except they took strong exception to my declaration that theirs was a different gospel and not a true form of Christianity. My concern was only for the impressionable young Christians whom they were trying to disciple away from our coffeehouse ministry. After my lecture the two cultists and I stood on the sidewalk in front of the coffeehouse and engaged in rather heated debate. Mostly they were offended that I said they were not Christians. They very much wanted the ministers of that city to embrace them as just another Christian denomination and not as a sect or cult. I tried to explain to them and the two or three dozen listeners standing around that I loved them and did not hate them, but that I could not affirm their beliefs as Christian or their movement as an authentically Christian one.

Suddenly a pickup truck screeched to a halt in front of the coffeehouse, stopping right where I stood arguing with the two cult leaders. A man I recognized as steeped in folk religion jumped out, listened for a minute, and then grabbed me and my two conversation partners by the arms. "Do you love Jesus?" he asked us each intently. We all affirmed that we did. Then he said loudly, "Then stop arguing and just love each other!"

Like too many Christians this man had little interest in truth; his only real interest was in warm, fuzzy experiences of God and of love. (I knew him well; he was just such a person who always resisted any kind of doctrinal or intellectual examination of faith.) It was clear that he felt I was inappropriately judging the two men in clerical robes with huge metal crosses hanging down their chests on necklaces. I was disheartened by

> **IF** Christianity is compatible with anything and everything, it is meaningless.

his move; it undermined everything I was trying to do to protect our young Christians and spiritual seekers from falling into this heretical sect. I believe what I was doing was appropriate judging; if Christianity is compatible with anything and everything, it is meaningless.

BIBLICAL JUDGING

Jesus instructed his hearers in Matthew 7:1 not to judge. But what kind of judging was he forbidding? Surely not every kind. How do we know that? Because Jesus himself encouraged a kind of judging, and the entire New Testament refers to judging as important and necessary. In John 7:24 Jesus told his listeners, "Stop judging by mere appearances, but instead judge correctly." Did he contradict himself? Was he taking back what he said in the Sermon on the Mount (in Matthew 7)? I don't think so. Rather, he was talking about a different kind of judging.

When Jesus prohibited judging, he was talking about declaring people unsaved, which is God's prerogative alone. No doubt he was also condemning hypocritical judging. In John 7 he was talking about judging people's behavior. Some of his listeners were judging people's spirituality based on their law-keeping (Sabbath, circumcision, etc.). Jesus instructed them to be like God and judge people based not on outward appearances or acts but on their trust in him and on their character. In John 8:15 Jesus clarified by criticizing the Pharisees' standards of spirituality; they judged "by human standards." What did he mean? That they judged people's spiritual status by their conformity or lack of conformity to the Pharisees' own legalistic standards of morality and religiosity. Jesus did not condemn all judging but only improper judging. In fact, he said (in John 7) to judge by right judgment.

Paul the apostle provides another example of right and wrong judging. In Romans 2:1 he criticized some of his Christian readers for judging others when they were doing the very same things. In other words, he criticized hypocrisy. But was he opposed to all judging? Hardly. In 1 Corinthians 5:12–13 he wrote, "What business is it of mine to judge those outside the church? Are you not to judge those inside? God will judge those outside. 'Expel the wicked person from among you.'" In this passage we see bad judging condemned and another kind of judging commanded. Here Paul was telling Christians they should stop separating themselves from non-Christians and instead separate from people who call themselves Christians but live evil lives.

We know this by the context. Earlier in 1 Corinthians 5, Paul bemoaned the fact that the Corinthian church was condoning incest in the church; a man was living with his father's wife and engaging in sexual relations with her. Paul ordered them to "hand this man over to Satan for the destruction of the sinful nature so that his spirit may be saved on the day of the Lord" (v. 5). If that isn't judging I don't know what would be! I wonder what Paul would say to modern-day Christians who say, "Oh, you shouldn't judge like that!" (Probably something similar to what he would say to

Christians who say, "All sins are equal, you know!" as discussed in chapter 8.)

Throughout his ministry Jesus judged the legalism and judgmentalism of the Pharisees. Paul often harshly criticized other apostles and his own converts for falling away from the true gospel of grace or for living morally impure lives. He also condemned false doctrines. In his letter to the Galatians he went so far as to express his wish that those who troubled them with false teachings about circumcision would castrate themselves (Galatians 5:12)!

So what are we to conclude from these seemingly mixed New Testament messages about judging? First, there are different kinds of judging; some are appropriate and some are improper. Christians are not to condemn other people to hell. God is the only judge of people's eternal destiny. Moreover, Christians should not be like the Pharisees and judge people's spiritual lives by faulty criteria, such as whether they live according to human rules of conduct that have nothing to do with the gospel. Extrapolating from that, I think we can appropriately say "Judge not!" when we hear Christians criticizing other Christians just because they have different convictions about behaviors not clearly condemned in Scripture. For example, dancing and gambling are nowhere labeled sins in the Bible. I might express an informed opinion about whether they are good behaviors, but I shouldn't declare Christians who do them unspiritual or less than fully Christian.

Second, some judging is required by the New Testament; its appropriate setting is within the body of Christ, the church. Right judging is aimed at deciding whether certain behaviors and persons are Christian or not. Right now you might be saying, "Whoa! Hold on. I thought you said declaring people's eternal destiny is never right because that's God's business." I did and I stand by that. But there's a distinction between being a Christian and being saved. I know that's an unfamiliar distinction to many conservative Christians, but think about it. "Christian" means "Christ follower." A Christian is a disciple of Christ, a person who is growing in his or her walk with God through faith in Jesus Christ. Also, a Christian is someone who confesses certain essential beliefs about Jesus Christ such as his atoning death for our sins and his resurrection.

Let's return to the German theologian I mentioned earlier. He denied the bodily resurrection of Christ. Based on all that the New Testament says about how important that is (e.g., 1 Corinthians 15), I have to say he was no Christian (even though he was a minister of the German state church!). But I do not mean he is now in hell. That I do not know. God is the only judge of people's souls. And nowhere does the New Testament say that only Christians will be in heaven. All who call in repentance and faith on the Lord Jesus Christ will be saved whether they ever joined a Christian church or called themselves "Christians" or not.

Biblical judging, then, is following valid biblical criteria in deciding what beliefs and behaviors are Christian and sometimes whether people who claim to be Christian really are. In a recent interview in a major national news magazine, the president of the Church of Jesus Christ of the Latter-day Saints (Mormon) adamantly insisted that his church is Christian. Does that mean I must automatically accept that Mormons are Christians? Is everyone who claims to be Christian really Christian? How can that even be in our society with hundreds of different religious organizations claiming to be Christian, many of which believe in reincarnation or deny the deity of Jesus Christ or the Trinity?

While I certainly want to hold a "large tent" view of Christianity, there has to be some limits. The writer of 1 John declared that "every spirit that does not acknowledge Jesus is not from God" (4:3). The context makes clear that by this he means to expel from the church everyone who denies either Christ's deity or his humanity. The early Christians after the apostolic age followed John's lead and excommunicated heretics who denied either of these great truths because the entire gospel depends on them. Some of these second-century Christian leaders such as Polycarp knew John personally; they were trained in the faith by him. Polycarp's student Irenaeus taught what he heard Polycarp say about John.

These church fathers harshly judged people who called themselves Christians but denied Jesus Christ as truly God and truly human.

JUDGING, EVANGELISM, AND CHURCH DISCIPLINE

Almost every Christian and certainly all evangelicals affirm the importance of evangelizing the lost for Jesus Christ. But how can we preach the gospel to many unless we are convinced they need it? Therein lies a kind of judging. The great evangelists of history stood before crowds of people among whom they knew were people lost and destined for hell. They didn't claim to know exactly which of their hearers were in that condition, but they knew some were.

Jonathan Edwards and John Wesley led the Great Awakening revivals in England and America in the 1730s and 1740s. They preached fervently to sinners as well as to Christians and urged them to turn from their sins to accept Jesus as Savior and Lord. Sometimes they could be pretty judgmental. Edwards preached a famous sermon entitled "Sinners in the Hands of an Angry God," which helped spark one of the greatest revivals America has ever known. Wesley chastised Christians for being spiritually lazy and unconcerned about their and other people's souls. Every great evangelist and preacher has engaged in judging; where would we be without their reminders of repentance and holiness? Evangelism and church renewal have always depended on judging without judgmentalism. There is a difference. Condemning sin and calling for true repentance and amendment of life are what real evangelism has always been about, and the church has been filled and strengthened by them.

> **EVANGELISM** and church renewal have always depended on judging without judgmentalism.

Not only evangelism but church discipline depends on appropriate judging. This was discussed at length in chapter 8. Many Christians shy away from church discipline, which simply means holding Christians accountable for their lives. If they confess that they are Christ followers, they ought to be eager to live that way. Unfortunately, too often in the past churches have excommunicated members for such trivial offenses as dancing or drinking a glass of wine with a meal and have overlooked the more serious transgressions such as adultery, lying, dividing the church, and criticizing others without good cause. Because church discipline has been abused and is always difficult, most churches have abandoned it altogether. Also, we have succumbed to cultural accommodation; disciplining members appears to violate the American value of tolerance. The result is churches filled with people claiming to be Christians but holding false beliefs and living evil lives.

Jesus gave instructions on how to deal with this problem. In Matthew 18:15–20 he laid down some rules for handling sin (and we might add heresy) within the church. It is to be done carefully and in a spirit of love, but if a church member refuses to repent and stop living an evil, sinful lifestyle or teaching false doctrine, he or she should be treated as a "pagan or a tax collector" (15:17). In other words, the person should be excommunicated and the church should stand apart from him or her. The early radical reformers (Anabaptists) of the sixteenth century practiced the "ban," which was based expressly on this gospel passage. Members of their group were not to speak or have commerce with banned church members until and unless they repented. Some Anabaptist (Mennonite, Amish, and Hutterite) churches still practice this.

Less than a century ago most Protestant churches practiced a milder form of excommunication, whereby an unrepentant member could not participate in the sacrament of the Lord's Supper.

> **WITHOUT** some form of church discipline, which inevitably involves some kind of judging, the church becomes merely a social club without real meaning or purpose.

The only alternative to church discipline of some kind is having a mixed assembly of Christians and non-Christians within the church. Few evangelicals want that. Without some form of church discipline, which inevitably involves some kind of judging, the church becomes merely a social club without real meaning or purpose. Yet today's folk religion militates against church discipline. In the past it may have practiced it too stringently. Things have changed radically in a brief time span. Today the problem is invasion of Christian circles by the cultural individualism, relativism, and tolerance that pervades postmodern American society.

The solution is not a return to harsh, judgmental judging where people are excommunicated or publicly humiliated for minor infractions of social or church norms. We want no return of the Puritans' stocks! The solution is right judging along the lines of the New Testament—tough love that confronts and occasionally excludes in cases of serious heresy or evil living without repentance and life amendment.

DISCUSSION QUESTIONS

1. In what ways has American culture's emphasis on tolerance influenced the popularity of the saying "Judge not"? Do you agree that it did?

2. What do you think about individualism? What's good and what's bad about it? How has it affected your own life and spirituality?

3. Do you agree that Christians should never declare judgments about someone else's eternal destiny especially to hell? Can you ever be so sure about it as to say that an individual is going to hell or is in hell?

4. Do you agree that Christians ought occasionally to decide who is and who is not a Christian? Have you ever had to make such a decision? When and why? How did you decide?

5. What do you think about the distinction between "saved" and "Christian"? Can you see a value in that distinction? What is it? Or, do you think the distinction is bogus? Why?

6. After reading this chapter, do you have a different attitude toward judging than before reading it? How has your attitude changed? How will that affect your behavior?

material wealth
⟶ relative ?
- are we wealthy?

CHAPTER 10

MONEY ISN'T BAD, BUT ONLY WHAT WE DO WITH IT:

SO WHY DID JESUS SAY IT'S HARD FOR A RICH MAN TO ENTER HEAVEN?

A group of Christians sits together and talks about moral and ethical issues. Perhaps it is a Sunday school class or maybe a Wednesday evening Bible study at church. The subject of money arises and someone ventures a thought: "You know, it seems to me the Bible condemns seeking wealth. In Jesus' parables rich men were usually portrayed negatively. And the letter of James has some pretty harsh things to say about the rich and wealthy. Then there's Jesus' saying that it's easier for a camel to go through the eye of a needle than for a rich man to enter the kingdom of heaven. And, of course, the Bible says love of money is the root of all evil." An uncomfortable pause ensues. Then, predictably, someone else says, "I think it's not money that's bad or good but only what people do with it." There. The issue is settled. The majority of the mostly suburban, middle-class Christians agree and move on to another subject.

Maybe you haven't experienced this, but I have. Many times. Almost every time the issue of the Bible's sayings about wealth and money comes up in a Christian group setting, I can count on someone saying something like, "It isn't money that's bad or good but only what people do with it." That statement has taken on the status of a sacred cow in especially upper scale American Christian churches and groups. But that's not to say poorer Christians (and others) don't use it as well. The cliché can be heard in all kinds of settings where the subject of money and its spiritual implications comes under discussion. I would like to argue that it is an example of folk religion insofar as it functions as an unexamined conversation stopper rather than as a conclusion based on serious reflection meant to further the conversation about spirituality and money.

Like every other unexamined Christian cliché, this one needs to undergo biblical examination using the tools of reason, experience, and tradition. Especially if we are relatively affluent financially (or dependent on someone who is), our tendency might be to cling to this slogan to protect our vested interests. But as with everything else it should be subjected to the truth of God's revelation. Is money really morally neutral? Or is money spiritually toxic?

THE OLD TESTAMENT AND MONEY

Let's subject our cliché to some careful biblical analysis. "Money itself isn't bad or good but only what people do with it." Is that consistent with biblical revelation about money? The Old Testament presents us with some fairly ambiguous reflections about the subject. There's no systematic treatment of wealth there, but the Old Testament does show that many of the great patriarchs of Israel were quite wealthy, including notably Abraham. Abraham's descendent Joseph became a steward in the Egyptian king's household and eventually a leading government official there; every indication in the later chapters of Genesis shows that Joseph used tremendous wealth to help people in need. There is no condemnation of money or wealth there.

Throughout the Old Testament one finds a particular theme that God blesses his faithful people with abundance. This is called "deuteronomic theology"; God blesses his people with land and wealth so long as they worship him only and turn away from idols. An example of this theology may be found in Deuteronomy 11:13–17, which pronounces on the Hebrews blessings for obedience and curses resulting from unfaithfulness.

A more negative note about money begins to creep into the Bible in its wisdom literature (Psalms, Proverbs, etc.). Many of the sayings in Proverbs warn against the seductions of wealth and especially against the injustices of the wealthy:

- Wealth is worthless in the day of wrath, but righteousness [justice] delivers from death. (11:4)
- Those who trust in their riches will fall, but the righteous [just] will thrive like a green leaf. (11:28)
- Dishonest money dwindles away, but whoever gathers money little by little makes it grow. (13:11)
- The poor are shunned even by their neighbors, but the rich have many friends. It is a sin to despise one's neighbor, but blessed are those who are kind to the needy. (14:20–21)
- Whoever oppresses the poor shows contempt for their Maker, but whoever is kind to the needy honors God. (14:31)

The list of proverbs that addresses poverty and wealth could go on and on. In sum, the Bible's wisdom literature nowhere condemns money or wealth, but it does condemn oppression of the poor and counsels against putting desire for money and wealth above desire for wisdom and spirituality. "How much better to get wisdom than gold, to get insight rather than silver!" (16:16).

The book of Ecclesiastes is sometimes included with the Psalms and Proverbs as part of the Bible's wisdom literature. It's a strange book, as anyone who has read it knows. It is not written from the perspective of a spiritual person but from the perspective of a person without God who sees the futility of that kind of life. One theme of the book is the vanity of pleasure and wealth: "Better a poor but wise youth than an old but foolish king who no longer knows how to heed a warning" (Ecclesiastes 4:13).

THE Bible's wisdom literature nowhere condemns money or wealth, but it does condemn oppression of the poor and counsels against putting desire for money and wealth above desire for wisdom and spirituality.

Perhaps on the basis of Ecclesiastes the author of the well-known hymn "I'd Rather Have Jesus" should have written in the chorus, "than to be the king of a vast domain, *and* be held in sin's dread sway." The song is usually sung, "than to be the king of a vast domain, *or* be held in sin's dread sway." (I heard it both ways growing up!) "And" fits Ecclesiastes (and the whole biblical message about power and wealth) better than "or." Perhaps the song with "or" (as one usually sees it printed and hears it sung) might offend some rich and powerful people with its implication that "the king of a vast domain" might be a sinner. But who can deny it?

The Old Testament prophets spoke out against the powerful and wealthy who oppressed the poor. Amos, a lowly shepherd from the southern kingdom of Judah, went to the northern kingdom of Israel and preached against all kinds of evil and corruption there. He called the wealthy wives of the rich and powerful "cows of Bashan" because they oppressed the poor and crushed the needy (4:1). Through him God pronounced judgment on the elite of Israel "because you trample upon the poor and take from him exactions of wheat" (5:11 RSV). In Amos 8 God exhibits what looks like a temper tantrum against the wealthy who oppress the poor and includes a negative statement about money itself:

Hear this, you who trample the needy
    and do away with the poor of the land,
saying,
"When will the New Moon be over
    that we may sell grain,
and the Sabbath be ended
    that we may market wheat?"—
skimping on the measure,
    boosting the price
    and cheating with dishonest scales.... (Amos 8:4–5)

God was angry because all they thought about during the Sabbath and religious festivals was how to make more money even at the expense of the poor. Through the prophet God was saying that the rich of Israel plotted during worship how to get more money for less produce. God said he would never forget their deeds and he would make the land tremble because of it:

I will make the sun go down at noon
    and darken the earth in broad daylight.
I will turn your religious festivals into mourning
    and all your singing into weeping.
I will make all of you wear sackcloth
    and shave your heads.
I will make that time like mourning for an only son
    and the end of it like a bitter day. (Amos 8:9–10)

Clearly, the Old Testament shows that God hates injustice and oppression of the poor, and it warns against seeking wealth in order to make oneself great at the expense of others. However, nowhere does the Old Testament say that money or wealth is bad in and of itself. With only the Old Testament as guide the saying that money is neither bad nor good but only what you do with it might be able to stand unchallenged. However, the only time the powerful and wealthy are shown in a good light (especially in the prophets) is when they give to the poor and needy. Then they are counted among the righteous. But there is so much stern warning against misuse of wealth that one can rightly conclude from the Old Testament that wealth in and of itself constitutes a grave spiritual danger.

MONEY AND WEALTH IN THE NEW TESTAMENT

The New Testament deepens the Bible's overall negative image of wealth. In Luke's version of the Sermon on the Mount Jesus says, "Blessed are you who are poor, for yours is the kingdom of God" (Luke 6:20), and, "But woe to you who are rich, for you have already received your comfort" (6:24). Some have tried to argue that the "poor" in the Sermon are those who know their own sinfulness and need of forgiveness. Matthew calls them the "poor in spirit." But the context makes clear that Jesus also meant the poor in terms of material wealth. Jesus goes on after blessing them to warn those who are "full" and spoken well of that woe is coming to them. And he urges them to give liberally and to lend without expecting anything in return. The entire context indicates that the subject is wealth and oppression. Jesus is clearly speaking of the tremendous economic disparity in Israel and warning the rich to have regard for the poor.

In Mark 10:25 Jesus delivers the much debated saying, "It is easier for a camel to go through the eye of a needle than for the rich to enter the kingdom of God!" Several attempts to soften Jesus' statement have been offered up in favor of the wealthy. Some say, for example, that "camel" should really be translated "rope," based on some linguistic similarity between the two words in the original language. But does that make it any easier on the rich man? Is a rope going through the eye of a needle less miraculous than a camel going through it?

Others have suggested that the "eye of a needle" refers to a small gate in the wall of Jerusalem and that Jesus is using humor and irony as he points toward it and gives this saying. Even if that were true (which is doubtful), his point would still be the same—that wealth is a drag on spirituality.

Finally, many have pointed out that Jesus says, "All things are possible with God" (Mark 10:27), meaning that with God's help even a rich man can be saved. Is this supposed to get rich people off the hook? Obviously anyone can be saved if God wills it, but the impact of Jesus' saying cannot be softened no matter how hard we try. His point is that wealth is a hindrance to salvation. ⟵ *WHY?*

Several of Jesus' parables include characters who are rich, and they are uniformly bad. The same can be said of most of the stories in the Gospels that involve wealthy people. Yet, there can be no doubt that some rich people figure prominently in supporting Jesus and the early church. Joseph of Arimathea donates his burial cave for Jesus' interment. A group of wealthy women support Jesus financially (Luke 8:1–3).

The New Testament contains no blanket condemnation of wealth or rich people. It does, however, portray them in a largely negative light and warns against the seductions of money and wealth. In 1 Timothy 6 Paul writes:

> But godliness with contentment is great gain. For we brought nothing into the world, and we can take nothing out of it. But if we have food and clothing, we will be content with that. Those who want to get rich fall into temptation and a trap and into many foolish and harmful desires that plunge people into ruin and destruction. For the love of money is a root of all kinds of evil. Some people, eager for money, have wandered from the faith and pierced themselves with many griefs. (1 Timothy 6:6–10)

Matt 6:24

Doesn't this nicely sum up why Jesus said that it is hard for a rich man to enter the kingdom of heaven? Not because money is bad in and of itself but because, combined with our fallen human nature, it forms a combustible combination that usually explodes into greed and avarice.

One book of the Bible especially focuses on wealth and comes down hard on rich people. That's the letter of James — a book Martin Luther called an "epistle of straw." Over the years James has suffered from neglect especially among affluent Christians. The excuse often given is that it seems to elevate works over faith; that was Luther's reason for relegating it to a secondary status compared with Romans and Galatians. One has to wonder, however, whether James's statements about money and wealth might have something to do with the neglect of his warnings in many churches. Maybe it's not just that James puts rich people in a negative light but even more how strongly it does so. Listen to a portion of this letter, which is part of the inspired canon of Scripture:

> Listen, my dear brothers and sisters: Has not God chosen those who are poor in the eyes of the world to be rich in faith and to inherit the kingdom he promised those who love him? But you have dishonored the poor. Is it not the rich who are exploiting you? Are they not the ones who are dragging you into court? Are they not the ones who are blaspheming the noble name of him to whom you belong? (James 2:5–7)

The situation here is that rich people were being given special places of honor in the church; church members and leaders were fawning over them while ignoring the poor. This James condemns. But in the process of condemning it, he goes further and heaps abuse on rich people. In chapter 5 the apostle, often thought to be Jesus' brother, writes:

> Now listen, you rich people, weep and wail because of the misery that is coming on you. Your wealth has rotted, and moths have eaten your clothes. Your gold and silver are corroded. Their corrosion will testify against you and eat your flesh like fire. You have hoarded wealth in the last days. Look! The wages you failed to pay the workers who mowed your fields are crying out against you. The cries of the harvesters have reached the ears of the Lord Almighty. You have lived on the earth in luxury and self-indulgence. You have fattened yourselves in the day of slaughter. (James 5:1–5)

In the middle of this passage James condemns their oppression of workers so that many interpreters have used this passage to support the idea that wealth in and of itself is not bad, but only ill-gotten wealth. James, however, does not say that and treats all wealth as if it were ill-gotten.

The plain fact of the matter is that the Bible is rather hard on wealth and rich people. There's no getting around it. An examined, reflective faith must confront this fact and not turn aside from it or gloss over it with platitudes. Taken together, the Bible's testimony scattered throughout its pages is that abundance of money and wealth are spiritually dangerous and to be avoided. At the very least Christians should not seek to be wealthy but should live simple, humble lives of contentment with little.

> **THE** plain fact of the matter is that the Bible is rather hard on wealth and rich people. There's no getting around it.

CHRISTIANITY AND WEALTH

Throughout much of its history the Christian church has followed the biblical teaching about wealth, which can be summed up that wealth is spiritually pernicious; it has a tendency to hinder a person's relationship with God. Only rarely has the church condemned wealth or excluded rich people, which would be going further than the Bible goes. During the Middle Ages some Catholic groups (such as the "spiritual Franciscans," radical followers of Francis of Assisi) did condemn wealth and the wealthy. A few even went so far as to commit acts of terrorism against extravagantly rich people. By and large, however, the church taught the dangers of wealth even when some of its own leaders lived luxurious lives.

An early church father by the name of John Chrysostom (d. 407) preached and wrote against the Christian emperor and his court for wealth and power at the expense of the poor. Chrysostom is one of the ancient church's most highly revered spiritual leaders because he was a great preacher in Constantinople who dared to speak truth to power. He was nicknamed "Golden Mouth" (the meaning of "Chrysostom") because of his great preaching ability; the common people occasionally demanded that he continue preaching after he stopped. He was severely persecuted by the emperor for criticizing him and his court. In a famous homily, or sermon, on wealth, he wrote that "wealth is a wild beast: if it be tightly held it runs away: if it be let loose it remains where it is.... Disperse it then that it may remain with thee; bury it not lest it run away" (Homily II of Chrysostom's "Two Homilies on Eutropius").

Chrysostom did not condemn rich people, but he did criticize them for hoarding their wealth and praised those who gave up wealth in order to live an evangelical life of selfless devotion to God and others. Of wealth he wrote:

> Why dost thou hold it so tightly, when in the time of trial it profiteth thee nothing? If it has power when thou fallest into a strait, let it come to thy aid, but if it then runs away what need hast thou of it?... What profit was there in it? The sword was whetted, death was impending, an army raging: there was apprehension of imminent peril; and yet wealth was nowhere to be seen. Where did the runaway flee? It was itself the cause which brought about all these evils, and yet in the hours of necessity it runs away. (Homily II of Chrysostom's "Two Homilies on Eutropius")

In other words, wealth is ephemeral, fleeting, and useless in the hour of trouble. Why hold onto it so tightly?

Like Chrysostom most of the early church fathers gave up their money and possessions when they became Christians. Cyprian of North Africa was a rich and powerful Roman leader who converted to Christ in the early part of the third century. He gave all his wealth away to the poor and eventually died a martyr's death.

During the Protestant Reformation wealth once again became a subject of some controversy. Especially the radical Reformers, the Anabaptists, criticized wealth and called on their converts and followers to live simple lives of contentment. Luther and Calvin, on the other hand, were less vocal in their opposition to wealth, probably because they depended on princes and wealthy citizens to support their causes.

John Wesley (1703–1791) founded the Methodist movement in England and was instrumental in the revivals called the Great Awakening during the 1730s and 1740s. He noticed that when people came to Christ in conversion, they often experienced ensuing prosperity because of their renewed character and industry. No longer did they squander money on liquor and worldly pleasures; they invested it in starting small businesses and earned more money by working harder. They gained reputations for being honest and therefore reaped rewards of new customers and higher wages. Wesley was dubious about this unintended consequence of conversion because he also noticed that increased wealth tended to dampen the fires of spiritual fervor. His favorite maxim about money was "Earn all you can; save all you can; give all you can." Wesley and many other evangelical revivalists remarked on the ambiguous nature of money; it could help the cause of the gospel, but it also tended to make the wealthy greedy.

The testimony of the majority of spiritual Christian leaders throughout history is that money itself is neither good nor evil, but it tends to be a drag on spiritual vitality and often seduces people into greed. Until the rise of the so-called "prosperity gospel" in America in the 1970s, few Christian teachers ever considered great wealth a good thing. All that has changed. But even more, Christians with no particular sympathy with the charismatic gospel of health and wealth ("Name it and claim it!") have fallen into a lazy mentality about the subject and relied too easily and often on platitudes like "Money is neither good nor bad but only what you do with it."

Like virtually every other Christian cliché there is some truth in this one. Money is just metal or paper; in and of itself it has no moral value. It is morally neutral. The Christian wisdom of the ages, however, has regarded its accumulation as dangerous to one's spiritual health. I'm only in my fifties and yet I can remember

HAVE evangelical and other American churches succumbed to a materialistic, consumerist culture and abandoned the biblical and historical Christian disdain for wealth and material abundance? I think so.

when evangelical preachers and evangelists condemned "conspicuous consumption" as a sin. That means showing off one's wealth for the sake of drawing attention and making oneself look grand. Today this is rarely mentioned. Have evangelical and other American churches succumbed to a materialistic, consumerist culture and abandoned the biblical and historical Christian disdain for wealth and material abundance? I think so.

EXAMINED BELIEF ABOUT MONEY AND WEALTH

Because it is so often such a thought and conversation stopper, I'd like to call a moratorium on this slogan: "Money isn't bad or good but only what you do with it." In spite of its element of truth, it usually has the effect of truncating a healthy conversation about the dangers of wealth. Of course, if it is said to counter statements unequivocally condemning rich people just because they are rich, it has its place. But even then it should be followed by some conversation about what should be done with money and with wealth to make it good. For the most part, however, people who utter this cliché are trying to protect their own vested interests whether they're aware of that or not. Even if they aren't wealthy, they hope to be someday. After all, they might win the lottery! But in light of Scripture, is aspiring to win the lottery or to get rich in any way a good thing? Hardly. The Bible warns sternly against greed and avarice; wanting to be rich diverts people's attention away from spiritual things and toward material things.

Let's get more specific. I'd like to suggest that gambling in every form is incompatible with biblical Christianity. What do I mean by gambling? Some people immediately quibble that investing money in the stock market or buying shares in a mutual fund is a form of gambling. I don't agree. Real gambling is more than just taking a risk. All life involves risk insofar as it involves venture. There's a difference between the risk of investment and the risk of gambling. Gambling is when you use money to play a game that could result in your taking other people's money away from them. Even if it is with their consent (because they freely agreed to play the same game with you and others), it is still taking away their money, which often should be devoted to food or clothes for their children. Even lottery games fall into this category of gambling. Only greed motivates people to gamble.

There's no question of investing in the economy as in buying shares in a mutual fund. That enables companies to grow with the result that people get hired and the economy flourishes. Pure gambling seems incompatible with Christian virtue; it is in direct violation of 1 Timothy 6:6–10. What's strange, however, is that many Christian organizations that have ethical and behavioral codes for members of their communities stop short of prohibiting gambling. They often prohibit drinking alcohol or at least drunkenness. They often forbid sex outside of marriage as well as viewing pornography (if not R-rated movies!). But few even raise a moral or ethical question over gambling. Why? Is greed no longer a sin? Or have we decided it's just too hard to measure greed? But the same could be said of lust and drunkenness and lying.

The time has come for reflective Christians in America and everywhere to think again about money, wealth, and greed. We need to move from folk religion, which pours pat answers over questions raised about them, to examined faith, which dares to enter this issue's murky waters. I would like to argue that it is simply irrational to claim to be a Bible-believing Christian and participate without some feelings of guilt or at least hesitation in America's money-driven consumer culture.

What does it tell us when we see evangelical churches' parking lots crammed with expensive luxury cars? Is there possibly some correlation between that reality and the fact that hymns and songs about heaven are seldom, if ever, sung in those churches? When was the last time you heard a sermon on the joys of heaven?

Such songs and sermons were the bread and butter of evangelical churches of all kinds a century ago. But that was when most evangelical Christians lived simpler lives and few were wealthy or, as we now call it, "upper middle class." Affluence has glued our feet to this earth and deafened our souls to the noise of heaven.

But that's not the Bible's way, nor was it the way of Christians in general for almost two thousand years. Occasionally someone dares to raise the question of this lifestyle's spiritual validity. Almost always someone else becomes immediately defensive of money and wealth and says, "Money isn't bad or good but only what you do with it." That's too simplistic. The fact is that money has a way of seducing the human soul; there is never enough of it. Statistics show that overall and in general wealthy Christians give less of their income to charity than lower middle class and even poor Christians. Ask almost any pastor and he or she will tell you that the best givers are the elderly folks living on fixed incomes.

> **THE** fact is that money has a way of seducing the human soul; there is never enough of it.

I hope that the next time you hear someone say, "Money isn't bad or good but only what you do with it" (or something to that effect), you will gently challenge the slogan by asking what the Bible says about money and wealth and point your conversation partners to the letter of James. While some of what James says about the rich may be hyperbole, it nevertheless raises a big question mark over any pat endorsement of wealth as morally neutral.

Best are they convicts & comforts

DISCUSSION QUESTIONS

1. Have you ever heard this cliché that money isn't bad or good but only what's done with it? Did you believe that? What do you think about it after reading this chapter? Has it changed your attitude toward money? How?

2. How often have you heard the Bible's negative statements about money and wealth talked about in your church? Were you aware of these before reading this chapter? If not, why do you think that's the case?

3. Why do you think contemporary evangelical churches (and perhaps others as well) have broken from the long history of negative Christian attitudes toward wealth and money? Why is some version of the "prosperity gospel" so popular now?

4. Do you think that gambling is inherently wrong? Why or why not?

5. What overall impression of rich people has this chapter given you? How might your reading of this chapter affect your relationships with and ministry to any rich people you know?

6. After reading this chapter, what practical steps would you take with regard to money?

CONCLUSION:
BELIEVING WHILE LIVING WITH QUESTIONS

The purpose of this book has been pastoral. I said that at the beginning, and I hope you've caught the spirit in which it is written. By no means have I intended to tear down or ridicule anyone's beliefs. Even folk Christianity has value. It is certainly better than chronic skepticism or any number of false gospels among the cults and new religions. However, my concern is that too many Christians are stuck in folk religion and need to deepen their faith with reflection. What I tried to do in this book is to raise some important questions about just a few of the most prevalent Christian clichés. There are, of course, others that I could have included. But my hope is that by this time, you will "know the routine," as they say.

Take any unexamined religious slogan and put a question mark after it. Begin with an attitude of wonder. Is this really true? Is it partly true but partly false? Is it true in some contexts but not in others? Is it an overstatement? Is it biblical? Is it reasonable? Does it fit with lived experience? These are the crucial questions of examination applied to religious statements. All of this examination should be wrapped in an attitude of wonder, prayer, devout open-mindedness, and desire to grow and mature in faith.

> DEVELOPING an examined faith is a lifelong process; it can't be hurried.

Of course, folk religion, including folk Christianity, includes much more than just clichés. Merely by examining them one does not immediately or automatically grow beyond unexamined faith. This is just the beginning. Developing an examined faith is a lifelong process; it can't be hurried. But it can be helped along. This book has been an attempt to help it along.

The reflective Christian is one who questions what she believes while continuing to believe what she is questioning. At least she continues to believe the essence of the faith under examination even as some of its details have to be jettisoned. A major part of the process of developing a reflective faith is learning to distinguish between what is essential and what is not. The gospel is one thing; details of interpretation and application are something else. Too often people confuse them as if Christian belief were an all-or-nothing proposition.

> THE reflective Christian is one who questions what she believes while continuing to believe what she is questioning.

My hope and prayer is that you, the reader, will continue to believe the basic truths of Christianity that are struggling to come to expression in the ten slogans that form the chapters of this book. Each cliché communicates a truth in a distorted way. Folk religion swallows the distortion as well as the inner truth; reflective Christianity tries to separate them and hold onto the inner truth while questioning the way in which it is being communicated or believed. Often, the problem with the cliché is that it needs qualifying. It would be true given the proper biblically based, rationally necessary, and experientially required qualifications. Of course, our culture values sound bites, and that's the problem many people have with examined, reflective faith. It doesn't fit the format of sound bites or bumper stickers.

I can only hope that reading this little book of theology has put your feet onto the path of examined, reflective faith or has helped you continue on the path if you've already begun to walk it. The next step is to pick up a good book of basic Christian theology and read it. A good place to start is C. S. Lewis's *Mere Christianity*. Another one (I hope) is my own *The Mosaic of Christian Belief* (InterVarsity Press, 2002). Many others are published by Christian publishers such as Zondervan, Baker, InterVarsity, and Eerdmans. Good luck on your journey; go with God and with a sound community of believers around you. The journey should never be an isolated one.

We want to hear from you. Please send your comments about this book to us in care of zreview@zondervan.com. Thank you.

ZONDERVAN.com/
AUTHORTRACKER
follow your favorite authors

CPSIA information can be obtained at www.ICGtesting.com
Printed in the USA
LVOW081208070613

337410LV00001B/3/P